English for NSW

YEAR 8

— STAGE 4 —

Emily Beach

First published in 2024

Insight Publications Pty Ltd
3/350 Charman Road
Cheltenham Victoria 3192
Australia

Tel: +61 3 8571 4950
Email: books@insightpublications.com.au

www.insightpublications.com.au

English for NSW, Year 8, Stage 4 / Emily Beach

ISBN:

9781923016491

Edited by Lisa Neale

Cover by Melisa Paredes

Internal design by Federico Fonseca

Typesetting by Melisa Paredes

Printed by Markono Print Media Pte Ltd

CONTENTS

CONTENTS

UNIT 01

Standing on the shoulders of genres

Unit inquiry question:
How do narratives rework and combine elements of genre to create new, engaging texts?

In this unit, students will explore how **genres** can be combined in **narratives** to create new, engaging texts. Additionally, students will investigate aspects of **intertextuality**, considering how ideas and elements of genre can be reworked for different contexts and purposes. Students will closely explore the **style** of *A Monster Calls*, written by Patrick Ness and Siobhan Dowd and illustrated by Jim Kay. They will examine the ways in which the genres of gothic fiction, fantasy and fairy tale have been combined to create a new, **imaginative** narrative.

To address the focus inquiry question of the unit, students will engage with learning in three chapters:

Chapter 1

An introduction to genre

In this chapter, students will be introduced to the concept of genre. They will explore the genres of gothic fiction, fantasy and fairy tale. They will examine the features of each genre and identify these elements in a range of written and visual texts.

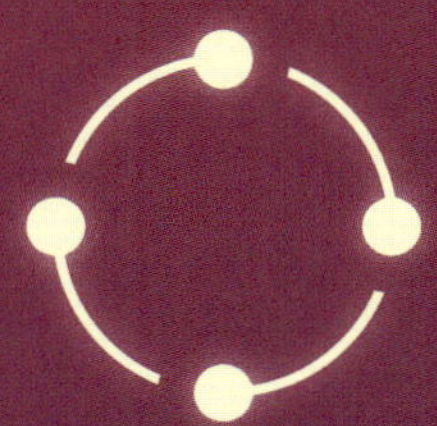

Chapter 2

Genres combined: *A Monster Calls*

In this chapter, students will examine the narrative style of *A Monster Calls* and the way it combines the three genres of gothic fiction, fantasy and fairy tale to create a new narrative. They will explore the way elements of the three genres have been transformed in the narrative to reflect important ideas and themes.

Chapter 3

Genre transformed

In this final chapter, students will craft their own narrative that combines elements of various genres and transforms one or more well-known narratives within these genres. Students will apply their understanding of the text features of imaginative writing.

The learning activities within each chapter and the summative assessment options (on pages 40-41) provide opportunities to assess student achievement of the following outcomes and content points.

Outcome and focus area	Content point
EN4-RVL-01 **Reading, viewing and listening to texts**	**Reading for challenge, interest and enjoyment**
	Read texts selected to challenge thinking, develop interest and promote enjoyment, to prompt a personal response Use strategies to enhance interest and overcome challenges experienced when reading Communicate purposefully with peers in response to texts Understand the ways reading helps us understand ourselves and make connections to others and to the world
EN4-URA-01 **Understanding and responding to texts A**	**Narrative**
	Understand narrative conventions, such as setting, plot and sub-plot, and how they are used to represent events and personally engage the reader, viewer or listener with ideas and values in texts, and apply this understanding in own texts Examine how narratives can depict personal and collective identities, values and experiences
EN4-URB-01 **Understanding and responding to texts B**	**Style**
	Describe and reflect on how particular arrangements of language features in texts can be found appealing according to personal preferences Understand how the style of a text can be the product of a particular time period, culture or genre
EN4-URC-01 **Understanding and responding to texts C**	**Genre**
	Understand how a genre addresses its purpose through patterns of textual elements, such as structure, choice of language, character archetypes and settings, and apply these patterns in own texts Analyse how texts can participate in larger, established patterns of narrative, purpose, theme and tone by exhibiting and challenging conventions, and experiment with conventions in own texts Explore particular genres to identify ways they may be adapted to different modes and media, or refreshed by combining with other genres, and experiment with these in own texts
	Intertextuality
	Analyse how texts can draw on elements of other texts to enrich meaning Understand how and why texts can be adapted, appropriated or transformed for different contexts, purposes and audiences, and experiment with adaptations, appropriations and transformations in own work

EN4-ECA-01	**Text features**
Expressing ideas and composing texts A	Use tense in a controlled manner that is appropriate for specific purposes Use imagery and figurative language to enhance meaning and create tone, atmosphere and mood, in a range of forms Compose texts that combine modes for intended purposes
	Text features: imaginative
	Compose texts that offer a cohesive consideration of thematic elements, including the development of a central complication or conflict Create imaginative texts using a range of language and structural devices to drive the plot, develop characters, and create a sense of place and atmosphere Experiment with unpredictable or unexpected structural features and explore how these can engage a reader Develop transformation skills by reshaping aspects of texts to create new meaning
	Sentence-level grammar and punctuation
	Control and experiment with aspects of syntax, including agreement, prepositions, articles and conjunctions to shape precise meaning and develop personal expression Apply punctuation conventions relevant to quotations and citing of sources Experiment with applying a wide range of punctuation to support clarity and meaning, and to control pace and reader response
	Word-level language
	Select effective, topic-specific vocabulary to enhance understanding and compose texts with accuracy, in a range of modes appropriate to audience, purpose, form and context Make vocabulary choices that draw on, or contribute to, stylistic features of writing and influence meaning

CHAPTER 1: AN INTRODUCTION TO GENRE

Chapter overview

In this chapter, you will be introduced to the concept of genre. You will explore the genres of gothic fiction, fantasy and fairy tale. You will examine the features of each genre and identify these elements in a range of written and visual texts.

Success criteria: in this chapter, I will be successful when I can ...

- describe the features of the gothic fiction, fantasy and fairy tale genres
- identify features of each genre in a range of written and visual texts
- explain the way features of genre are used to engage readers and reflect important ideas
- explain the connections between literary genres.

Chapter inquiry questions

- What is a literary genre?
- What are the features of gothic fiction?
- What are the features of fantasy?
- What are the features of fairy tale?

Key vocabulary

- genre
- gothic fiction
- fantasy
- fairy tale
- mythology
- intertextuality
- appropriation

What is a literary genre?

Texts can be grouped into categories that follow recognisable and identifiable patterns, also known as **genres**. Texts within a specific literary genre often share similar structures and identifiable features. Often, we come to have certain expectations when we engage with a particular genre. Studying genres helps us understand the relationships of texts within and between genres.

1.1.1 Warm-up

What would you expect to see in each genre?

For each literary genre or category of text listed below, identify a **character**, **setting** and **plot event** you would expect to see in a text within this genre.

The first genre has been completed for you.

Romance	**Adventure**
Character: *hopeless romantic* Setting: *Christmas holiday season* Plot event: *romantic chase and kiss scene*	Character: Setting: Plot event:
Crime fiction	**Fantasy**
Character: Setting: Plot event:	Character: Setting: Plot event:

Fiction genres are often categorised by their subject matter. Some examples of genre include science fiction, crime fiction, romance, fantasy and speculative fiction. However, some narratives combine genres to appeal to broader audiences and challenge traditional expectations of genre.

As this unit continues, we will explore the genres of gothic fiction, fantasy and fairy tale and the way they have been combined in the narrative *A Monster Calls*. But first, let's understand the history and identifiable features of each genre.

What are the features of gothic fiction?

DISCUSS

What do you think of when you see the word 'gothic'? Discuss with a small group.

The genre of **gothic fiction**, a precursor to the modern-day horror genre, arose in the late eighteenth century as part of the Romantic movement in the arts. The genre was given its name because much of its inspiration was drawn from medieval buildings and cathedrals, many of which are gothic in architectural style. Horace Walpole's novel *The Castle of Otranto* (1764) is believed to have been the first gothic novel written. Other famous writers of gothic fiction include Edgar Allan Poe ('The Raven'), Mary Shelley (*Frankenstein*) and Bram Stoker (*Dracula*).

Gothic fiction often explores dark themes and emotional extremes. Let's explore some of the features that distinguish this genre of literature.

Setting: gothic stories are often set in dark places, such as cemeteries, caves or dungeons, or places that have been neglected, such as the ruins of buildings, castles, churches or country manors.

Foreboding atmosphere and tension: the genre aims to create an emotional response in readers, and to do so relies on maintaining tension. Often a foreboding, threatening or ominous atmosphere is also sustained throughout the story.

The supernatural: the presence of supernatural or other-worldly elements is a key feature of this genre. This may include unexplained phenomena such as ghosts, monsters or apparitions.

Flawed, lonely protagonist: the main character (protagonist) of a gothic story often experiences a sense of isolation and loneliness, as a result of either their own choices or those of others. The protagonist may be an outcast from society in some way.

Heightened emotions: characters in gothic texts are often characterised by heightened emotional states. These are often associated with fear, grief, loss or death.

A writer in the gothic fiction genre during the nineteenth century was Edgar Allan Poe. You will now examine part of one of his most famous works, a poem called 'The Raven' (1845). See if you can recognise the features of gothic fiction listed above in the extract from the poem.

In this poem, the narrator is upset about the death of a woman named Lenore, and one night he is visited by a raven. Ravens are known to symbolise death but are also associated with sharing wisdom and important lessons. Let's read the opening of the poem.

The Raven

by Edgar Allan Poe (1845)

Once upon a midnight dreary, while I pondered, weak and weary,
Over many a quaint and curious volume of forgotten lore –
While I nodded, nearly napping, suddenly there came a tapping,
As of some one gently rapping, rapping at my chamber door.
'Tis some visitor,' I muttered, 'tapping at my chamber door –
Only this and nothing more.'

Ah, distinctly I remember it was in the bleak December;
And each separate dying ember wrought its ghost upon the floor.
Eagerly I wished the morrow; – vainly I had sought to borrow
From my books surcease of sorrow – sorrow for the lost Lenore –
For the rare and radiant maiden whom the angels name Lenore –
Nameless *here* for evermore.

INTERPRET

Circle examples of words that help to create a negative or dark image.

INTERPRET

Read the opening of the poem aloud. You will notice that the rhyme scheme for the poem is ABCBBB. Discuss with a small group the effect of this rhyme scheme. How does it add to the foreboding atmosphere?

1.1.2 Understanding and responding to texts C

1 How does Poe establish a foreboding atmosphere in the opening of his poem 'The Raven'? Give evidence from the poem to support your response.

2 What have you learned about the narrator from the opening of this poem? How might the narrator be a gothic character? Give evidence from the poem to support your response.

3 What other gothic features do you think will be featured in this poem? What evidence do you have that supports your suggestion?

What are the features of fantasy?

DISCUSS

What's the best fantasy text you have read or viewed? Discuss with a small group.

The **fantasy** genre has its origins in the sharing of folk tales and fairy tales. Many of these traditional stories have fantasy elements. Additionally, the genre is heavily influenced by stories from **mythology**.

However, the genre has evolved since the sharing of folk tales, fairy tales and myths, and modern fantasy is recognised as a genre of its own. Some famous works of early modern fantasy include *Alice's Adventures in Wonderland* by Lewis Carroll (1865), *The Hobbit* by J.R.R. Tolkien (1937) and *The Chronicles of Narnia* series by C.S. Lewis (1950–1956). In more recent times, the *Harry Potter* series by J.K. Rowling (1997–2007) has created even more interest in the genre.

Let's explore some of the features that characterise this genre of literature.

VOCABULARY

mythology
noun: the sharing of myths, mostly concerning the early history of a people or explaining a natural or social occurrence.

Magic and wonder: writers of fantasy experiment with as many imaginative qualities as they can to create magic and wonder. Magical elements may include witches, monsters, dragons, talking animals or magical objects. Although magic provides an escape from reality, the characters of fantasy stories must still deal with very human emotions and experiences.	
Quest and adventure: essential to a fantasy story is quest and adventure. The main character (protagonist) must embark on a journey, usually physical in nature, to achieve a goal or ambition. However, the protagonist will encounter challenges and obstacles in this journey. The quest becomes more than just a physical journey; instead, the protagonist will learn important lessons about themselves.	

Imaginative setting: fantasy settings often blur the line between reality and imagination, through parallel worlds. Settings may include imagined places, medieval societies or enclosed worlds, like a secret forest or a planet.	
Hero protagonist: the fantasy hero is often in conflict with themselves and must learn to grow and change throughout the quest that they must undertake. The hero is often guided by a mentor who provides wisdom and support throughout the quest.	
Battle between good and evil: most fantasy stories build towards an epic battle, usually a physical conflict, to resolve an issue or allow the hero to achieve justice.	

Now let's recognise some of these features in fantasy texts.

Dragon Hunter

by Nazam Anhar

The battle with the dragons had taken place so long ago – hundreds, or maybe thousands of years – that few people in the village still believed in it. Most said the stories of the dragons were only legends handed down from ancient times, only fireside tales fit for the ears of children and fools. 'When the dragons come again' was a common saying in the village, used when speaking of something that would never happen, or a time that would never come.

... Baran had few friends in the village. He had no father – he had died when Baran was very young. He lived with his mother and two younger sisters. In his village, a boy without a father to provide for him, and teach him the skills that a man must know to make his way in the world was treated as an outcast. What made things even worse for Baran was that his father had not been a native of Shenzing. He was from the tribe of Rovers, the people who lived in tents, wandering endlessly to find good grazing for their lean cattle ... The most awful thing about the Rovers, the villagers thought, was that they practised the dark arts of witchcraft.

... As he stood watching the winged creatures in the sky, Baran suddenly felt sure, in a way that was strangely thrilling as well as frightful, that the old stories of the dragon raids were true ... Baran had to warn the others of the danger as quickly as he could. He turned and began racing down the mountainside towards the valley.

... 'Dragons!' he cried out to them. 'The dragons are coming!'

The farmers looked up at him, shook their heads, and went on with their work as if they had not heard.

1.1.3 Reading texts

1 Complete the 'See, Think, Wonder' learning routine below in response to the *Dragon Hunter* extract. In a small group, share your responses.

SEE What features of fantasy do you see?	THINK What do you think will happen next in the text?	WONDER What do you wonder about the way this text is written?

2 Identify *two* features of the fantasy genre in this extract. Give evidence from the text to support your response.

Fantasy feature	Textual evidence

3 What physical quest do you think Baran will need to undertake? What emotional journey do you think he will also take on this physical adventure?

Find and watch the trailers for the following films online.

Harry Potter and the Philosopher's Stone (2001)

The Golden Compass (2007)

Alice in Wonderland (2010)

1.1.4 Understanding and responding to texts C

1 What do the main characters in these films have in common? Give evidence from the film trailers to support your response.

2 What do these characters' quests have in common? Give evidence from the film trailers to support your response.

Extension activity

As referenced earlier, fantasy stories can be heavily influenced by mythology. Some fantasy stories may even include intertextual references to mythological stories.

In small groups, research and discuss some fantasy stories that are inspired by mythology. Consider how the stories compare and what each new story adds to the original myth.

VOCABULARY

intertextuality
noun: when a text draws on or refers to another text. References to another text can be obvious but they can also be made through other features such as characters or storylines.

What are the features of fairy tales?

A **fairy tale** is a type of story within both the fantasy and folklore genres. Fairy tales are some of the oldest stories that exist, originating from many cultures and time periods.

DISCUSS

Discuss with a small group the fairy tales you most clearly remember from your childhood. Are there any differences between your group members in the way you remember the stories?

Many fairy tales date back many centuries and were originally told orally (through the spoken word) to share important messages and lessons. Although they were originally created for and shared among adults, fairy tales evolved to be mostly written for children.

In 1812, many of the traditional Western fairy tales we know were collected and published in Germany by the Grimm brothers. Some of the fairy tales they included were 'Cinderella', 'Hansel and Gretel', 'Rapunzel', 'Sleeping Beauty' (published as 'Briar Rose') and 'Little Red Riding Hood'.

Standing on the shoulders of genres

Fairy tales are magical stories that follow a traditional structure, usually beginning with 'Once upon a time ...' Let's examine the other main features of this genre.

Magic: as the name suggests, fairy tales have a magical dimension. This may be mythical or magical characters, such as witches, elves and fairies, or magical events that occur within the story.

Clearly defined characters: fairy tales often feature clearly defined characters – usually those who are 'good', like the hero of the story, and those who are 'bad', like the villain. Fairy tales are often set in the past but not in a specific time period, so these characters show that some elements of human nature are timeless.

Task and obstacles: the central character will often need to solve a problem or undertake a specific task to restore order. Of course, there are challenges in this process that the character must overcome.

Moral lessons: although the main aim of fairy tales is entertainment, the other significant aim is to share an important moral lesson. The fairy tale might be symbolic of a broader issue, with the moral of the story reflecting a value that is important to society.

Resolution and closure: we've all heard the phrase '... and they all lived happily ever after'. The ending of a fairy tale provides closure for readers once order and good have been restored.

1.1.5 Understanding and responding to texts C

In a small group, select a well-known fairy tale. Find a copy of this story online and read it aloud together.

In the table below, record examples of the key features from your selected fairy tale.

Fairy tale title: ____

Key fairy tale features	Examples from the selected fairy tale
Magic	
Clearly defined characters	
Task and obstacles	
Moral lessons	
Resolution and closure	

Traditionally, fairy tales are universal and timeless, which means that the events of the story could happen in any society or time period. However, fairy tales are now often **appropriated**, which means they are re-created for a new context with their overall message changed to reflect the concerns of the new setting, time or society.

VOCABULARY

appropriation
noun: occurs when an element of an original text (like characters or plot) is used in a new text in a different context.

1.1.6 Understanding and responding to texts C

'Mirror, mirror on the wall ...'

1 Find the original fairy tale of 'Snow White' online and read a scene containing this famous line.

2 Find and watch *two* film versions of this same scene online. Some examples include:

- *Snow White and the Seven Dwarfs* (1937)
- *Shrek* (2001)
- *Mirror Mirror* (2012)

3 Complete the Venn diagram below to compare how the texts use this line to create meaning.

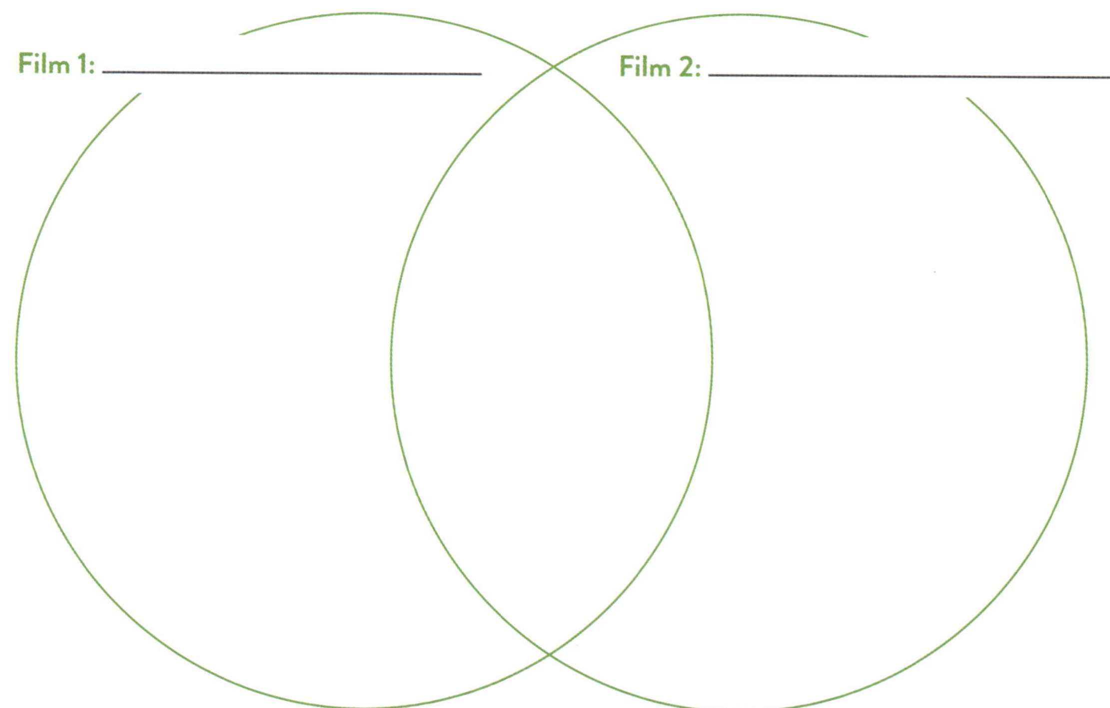

1.1.7 Chapter reflection

In this chapter, you have been introduced to the concept of **genre** and have examined the key features of gothic fiction, fantasy and fairy tales.

1 Summarise your understanding of each of the genres examined in this chapter.

Genre	Your understanding
Gothic fiction	
Fantasy	
Fairy tale	

2 What connections can you make between these genres?

3 Let's return to this unit's inquiry question: ***How do narratives rework and combine elements of genre to create new, engaging texts?*** How have your learning and reading experiences in Chapter 1 addressed the inquiry question?

CHAPTER 2:

GENRES COMBINED: *A MONSTER CALLS*

Chapter overview

In this chapter, you will examine the narrative style of *A Monster Calls* and the way it combines the three genres of gothic fiction, fantasy and fairy tale to create a new narrative. You will explore the way elements of the genres have been transformed in the narrative to reflect important ideas and themes.

Success criteria: in this chapter, I will be successful when I can ...

- describe the narrative style of the novel *A Monster Calls*
- describe the features of the gothic fiction, fantasy and fairy tale genres in *A Monster Calls*
- explain how the combining of genres contributes to the unique style of the narrative.

Chapter inquiry questions

- What is the narrative style of *A Monster Calls*?
- How are genres combined to create a dark, mythical reality?
- How are genres combined to reveal Conor's monstrous quest?

Key vocabulary

- narrative
- style
- motif
- allegory
- symbolism

What is the narrative style of A Monster Calls?

A Monster Calls is a 2011 novel written by Patrick Ness and Siobhan Dowd and illustrated by Jim Kay. The original idea for the novel came from Siobhan Dowd, who died of cancer before she could write the story. It tells the story of Conor, who has been having nightmares ever since his mother started cancer treatment. Conor is visited by a monster who tells him that he wants the most dangerous thing of all from Conor: the truth. We discover that it is not the monster that Conor is afraid of, but rather confronting the events of his recurring nightmare and the truth of his reality.

1.2.1 Warm-up

What's in a front cover?

Search online for an image of the front cover of *A Monster Calls* by Patrick Ness, Siobhan Dowd and Jim Kay. What features of each genre can you identify in this front cover image?

Gothic fiction	Fantasy	Fairy tale

DISCUSS

First, use the QR code to find and read the article 'Patrick Ness: Why I wrote *A Monster Calls*'.

With a small group, discuss Ness' comments on the target audience of the novel. How and why do you think children and adults react differently to the novel?

Remember, the function of a **narrative** goes beyond just the structure of the text. A narrative can depict personal and shared experiences, helping to comment on important topics. When a text such as *A Monster Calls* reflects confronting themes such as death and loss, there can be discussion about whether it is suitable for its young adult audience.

- What are your thoughts on whether confronting themes belong in young adult novels?
- How do you think the novel *A Monster Calls* provides hope for its readers?

1.2.2 Expressing ideas and composing texts A

Style refers to the characteristic ways in which a composer chooses to express their ideas. Style can be a product of a particular time period, culture or genre. As readers, we may favour particular styles, but we can also learn to appreciate a variety of different styles.

Below are some of the most significant aspects of the narrative style of *A Monster Calls*.

First person narration: the novel is mostly narrated in the first person from the perspective of Conor. (The settings of the text are also places personal to Conor: his bedroom, his school, his grandmother's house and the hospital.)
1 Why do you think first person narration has been chosen? __________ __________
Fragmented structure: the chapters of the novel are short and move quickly between locations and events.
2 How do you think this fragmented style might reflect how Conor is feeling at this point in his life? __________ __________

Symbolism: there are many objects, people and events that symbolise important moral lessons for Conor. For example, the monster's stories all symbolise something greater than their literal events.

3 What symbol can you think of that could reflect fear? Draw a picture here and discuss it with a partner.

Two other significant aspects of style in *A Monster Calls* are the novel's illustrations and the way reality and fantasy are blurred together. These aspects will be explored in more depth as this chapter continues.

A key part of the unique style of *A Monster Calls* is the way the genres of gothic fiction, fantasy and fairy tale are combined to create the narrative. Let's examine how important aspects of this text are created by combining these genres to engage audiences.

How are genres combined to create a dark, mythical reality?

The novel combines the genres of gothic fiction and fantasy to create a dark, mythical reality that allows Conor to escape the fears he has about his situation and learn to process his grief. The opening of the novel quickly establishes a foreboding and eerie atmosphere, characteristic of the gothic fiction genre. An atmosphere of tension is also created as readers are made to feel a sense of impending danger and anticipation from the opening, unsure of what will happen to Conor.

Read the opening of the novel, considering how setting and atmosphere are established.

A Monster Calls

by Patrick Ness and Siobhan Dowd, illustrated by Jim Kay

LANGUAGE

Circle examples of sensory imagery (references to what Connor can see, hear or feel).

INTERPRET

Identify and label examples of the gothic fiction and fantasy genres in this extract.

The monster showed up just after midnight. As they do.

Conor was awake when it came.

... He listened, straining against the silence, but all he could hear was the quiet house around him, the occasional tick from the empty downstairs or a rustle of bedding from his mum's room next door.

Nothing.

And then something. Something he realised was the thing that had woken him.

Someone was calling his name.

Conor.

... Then he heard a heavy creak of wood outside, as if something gigantic was stepping across a timber floor.

... Wide awake now, he pushed back the covers, got out of bed, and went over to the window. In the pale half-light of the moon, he could clearly see the church tower up on the small hill behind his house, the one with the train tracks curving beside it, two hard steel lines glowing dully in the night. The moon shone, too, on the graveyard attached to the church, filled with tombstones you could hardly read any more.

... A cloud moved in front of the moon, covering the whole landscape in darkness, and a *whoosh* of wind rushed down the hill and into his room, billowing the curtains.

... Then the cloud passed, and the moon shone again.

On the yew tree.

Which now stood firmly in the middle of his back garden.

And here was the monster.

1.2.3 Understanding and responding to texts B and C

1 Describe Ness' writing style in the opening of the novel. What do you notice about his use of language to create the setting?

______

______

______

2 How is this opening characteristic of the gothic fiction genre?

______

______

______

Although the setting is typical of the gothic fiction genre, the novel also begins with the moment the monster first appears at Conor's house, which suggests to readers that it will play a significant role in Conor's life and transformation. The monster is a supernatural or mythical being, an element that occurs in all three genres introduced in this unit. With the introduction of the monster, the line between reality and fantasy is instantly blurred.

The **illustrations** in this novel contribute to the unique style of the text and help readers visualise the way the monster, a mythical being, coexists with Conor in reality. A black and white, hand-drawn style is used for the illustrations by Jim Kay, reflecting both the gothic, eerie atmosphere and the 'grey area' between what is real and what is fantasy.

1.2.4 Understanding and responding to texts B

Examine the illustrations from the novel and the accompanying text below.

Conor whirled around. Somehow, some way, the monster was in his grandma's sitting room. It was far too big, of course, having to bend down very, very low to fit under the ceiling, its branches and leaves twisting together tighter and tighter to make it smaller, but here it was, filling up every corner.

1 Describe the style of the illustrations.

2 How do the illustrations show the way the real world and fantasy exist together?

3 What do you think the text shows about what Conor must learn to accept?

4 Search online for the 'Lunch Room' scene from the 2016 film adaptation of *A Monster Calls* (directed by J.A. Bayona). Discuss with a group how this scene continues to show how the monster exists in Conor's world.

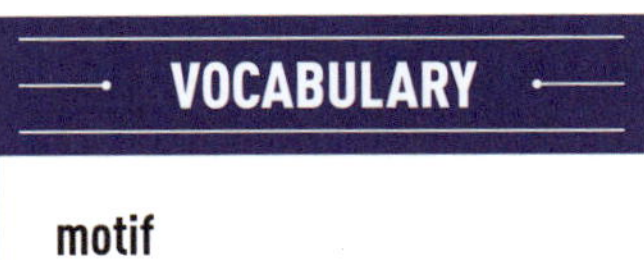

VOCABULARY

motif
noun: a recurring idea, object, symbol or phrase in a text that reflects its broader ideas and themes.

Another significant aspect of the style of this narrative that contributes to the blurring between reality and fantasy is the **motif** of time.

1.2.5 Understanding and responding to texts B

The monster always visits Conor at 12:07, which we later learn is the time at which his mother dies at the end of the text.

What does this motif symbolise about what Conor must learn to accept about time in his process of grieving?

How are genres combined to reveal Conor's monstrous quest?

Central to the genres of fantasy and fairy tale is a quest that the main character must embark on to achieve a goal or ambition. Conor's quest in the novel is an emotional one, through which he must learn that his mother's death is inevitable and he must learn to accept her passing. While Conor is initially presented as a gothic protagonist who has isolated himself from the world, we come to discover that he also displays qualities of a typical fantasy hero who undergoes a quest for acceptance. The 'hero's journey' is a key feature of both the fantasy and fairy tale genres.

DISCUSS

Engage in your own research online about the stages of the 'hero's journey', often represented in the fantasy and fairy tale genres. Create a timeline to reflect these stages. You could also plot events from a well-known text, such as *Harry Potter* or *The Lord of the Rings*, on your timeline to demonstrate your understanding of the hero's journey. Which stages of the hero's journey are evident in what you know of Conor's story from this chapter so far?

The monster is introduced as a spiritual mentor to guide Conor through the journey of grief to acceptance. Although he is named 'the monster', which is a nice **intertextual reference** to the early gothic novel *Frankenstein* by Mary Shelley, we learn that the character is actually to be both feared and admired. Conor even tells the monster he isn't afraid of him; rather, we learn that he is afraid of admitting that he is ready to let his mother go.

The yew tree, from which the monster is made, is deeply **symbolic**. It has mythological meaning as a symbol of rebirth and everlasting life.

DISCUSS

Research the mythology of the yew tree. Discuss the link between the tree and ancient healing practices.

Although Conor initially believes the monster has come from the yew tree to signal his mother's healing, we learn that it is Conor who must be healed instead. Read the following extract, in which Conor learns that his mother's new treatment is a drug made from yew trees.

> Unless the monster was here for a reason. Unless it had come walking to heal Conor's mother.
>
> He hardly dared hope. He hardly dared *think* it.
>
> No.
>
> No, of course not. It couldn't be true, he was being stupid. The monster was a dream. That's all it was, a *dream*.
>
> But the leaves. And the berries. And the sapling growing in the floor. And the destruction of his grandma's sitting room.
>
> Conor felt suddenly light, like he was somehow starting to *float* in the air.
>
> Could it be? Could it really be?
>
> He heard voices and looked down the corridor. His dad and his grandma were fighting.

1.2.6 Reading texts

1 Describe the tone of this extract. What does this suggest about how Conor is feeling?

2 Why have some words been italicised in the extract?

3 What does the final line of the extract tell you about what may happen next?

The monster shares tales with Conor to help him learn to accept his mother's inevitable death. These tales become a characteristic element of the novel's style. They are **allegories**, like fairy tales, that reflect important moral lessons for Conor.

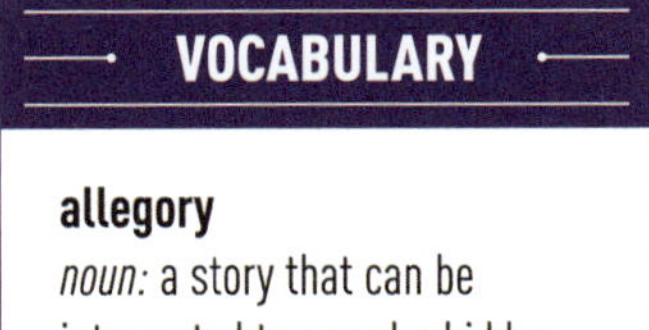

allegory
noun: a story that can be interpreted to reveal a hidden meaning, typically a moral meaning.

1.2.7 Understanding and responding to texts B

1 Read the summary of each tale in the table below. Explain the moral lesson of each one.

	What do you think is the moral lesson that Conor must learn?
First tale In an ancient village, it is assumed that a wicked queen has killed a farmer's daughter because she is loved by the prince. However, Conor learns that the prince is the villain, and the wicked queen isn't wicked after all.	

Second tale An apothecary requires a yew tree to make medicine, but a parson (whose land the yew tree grows on) doesn't let him take it. When the parson's daughters then become sick, the apothecary refuses to give him medicine and his daughters die.	
Third tale The monster meets a man who is invisible, but in reality, the people around him have just become so used to overlooking him that they don't see him anymore. One day he becomes tired of being unseen.	

2 Instead of telling a fourth tale, the monster asks Conor to tell the story of his nightmare: letting go of his mother's hand. Why is this significant for Conor's journey towards acceptance?

1.2.8 Chapter reflection

1 Explain how the combining of genres contributes to the unique style of this narrative.

2 Let's return to this unit's inquiry question: ***How do narratives rework and combine elements of genre to create new, engaging texts?*** How have your learning and reading experiences in chapter 2 addressed the inquiry question?

CHAPTER 3: GENRE TRANSFORMED

Chapter overview

In this final chapter of the unit, you will compose your own text that combines elements of the genres you have studied and transforms one or more well-known narratives. You will apply your understanding of the text features of imaginative writing to engage your readers and convey ideas.

Success criteria: in this chapter, I will be successful when I can ...

- identify aspects of well-known narratives within each genre that can be appropriated for a new audience
- combine genre styles to create character voice
- experiment with written language to create and maintain atmosphere.

Chapter inquiry questions

- How can I appropriate the ideas of well-known texts for my own audience?
- How can I combine genres to create character in my own text?
- How can I combine genres to create setting and atmosphere in my own text?

Key vocabulary

- appropriation
- atmosphere
- syntax
- vocabulary
- imagery
- figurative language
- values

How can I appropriate the ideas of well-known texts for my own audience?

In this chapter, you will be guided to write your own **appropriation** of one or more well-known narratives, combining elements of the gothic fiction, fantasy and fairy tale genres. Your imaginative piece is to be written for a contemporary, modern audience. You will be guided in developing the plot, writing with character voice and creating atmosphere in a setting.

VOCABULARY

appropriation
noun: occurs when an element of an original text (like characterisation or plot) is used in a new text in a different context.

1.3.1 Warm-up

Another tale ...

You've read about the tales told to Conor by the monster in *A Monster Calls*. Compose another tale that could be shared by the monster, inspired by a well-known fairy tale. Consider what you may change about the original fairy tale to ensure that it is relevant for Conor.

Now that you are an expert in the genres of gothic fiction, fantasy and fairy tale, it is time for you to experiment writing imaginatively within these genres. However, just as Patrick Ness combined these genres in *A Monster Calls*, you will also be inspired by the genres to create your own character and setting.

First, let's consider how you can be inspired by well-known texts within each genre. You will plan how you can appropriate a text for a new, modern audience.

1.3.2 Expressing ideas and composing texts A

1 Get inspired! Find novel excerpts (or summaries) or film trailers for some of the texts listed below in each genre. Engage with a few texts in each genre.

Gothic fiction	Fantasy	Fairy tales
The Graveyard Book (novel) *Coraline* (film) *Dracula* (novel) *Corpse Bride* (film)	*The Book of Dust* (novel series) *Onward* (film) *The Fire Star* (novel) *The Lion, the Witch and the Wardrobe* (film)	*Ye Xian* (Chinese fairy tale) *Shrek* (film) *Mufaro's Beautiful Daughters* (African fairy tale) *Maleficent* (film)

2 Now that you have read and viewed a range of texts across the genres, you will plan how you will appropriate one or more of these texts, combining their genres to create an idea for your own text for a modern audience. You will use the SCAMPER technique to plan your appropriation. This is a brainstorming tool that can be used to help appropriate or rethink an existing text.

Chosen text/s: ______________________________

SCAMPER	Record your ideas
Substitute What can you replace so that the story works better for your audience?	
Combine What elements of other genres can you combine to create a new text?	
Adapt What can you reshape for a new audience?	
Modify What part could be made smaller or bigger to reveal something different?	
Purpose What needs to change so that the text can achieve a new purpose?	

Eliminate What parts can be removed that are no longer relevant?	
Reverse What events can be ordered differently to change the meaning or impact?	

3 With a partner, discuss the ideas you have for an imaginative piece that combines the genres of gothic fiction, fantasy and fairy tale. How was this inspired by the texts you have read or viewed in this unit? Give each other feedback on how the new, appropriated story will appeal to a modern audience.

4 It is important that you also carefully consider the purpose or overall idea for your text. What is the overall idea that you want your text to communicate?

______

______

______

5 Bearing in mind the feedback from your partner and the overall idea of your text, write a brief summary of the plot events of your own imaginative piece that appropriates a well-known narrative. Consider how you can experiment with unpredictable or unexpected structural features.

______

______

______

______

______

How can I combine genres to create character in my own text?

One of the most important ingredients in any imaginative text is character. Readers will connect with your character and hopefully build a relationship with them as your text progresses. You can reveal important ideas through your character's voice, and may also challenge readers to see the world differently. The way a character responds to certain events and experiences will reveal their beliefs and **values**.

> **VOCABULARY**
>
> **values**
> *noun:* individual beliefs or principles that motivate a person's behaviour and actions. For example, honesty, loyalty, justice, search for truth.

In this part of the chapter, you will create a character for your imaginative appropriation. You may modify an existing character or create a character of your own that combines elements of the three genres.

1.3.3 Expressing ideas and composing texts A

1 Return to Chapter 1 and revise the typical characters of each genre. Consider how you can be inspired by these character types and complete the table below to begin planning your character.

	Gothic fiction	Fantasy	Fairy tale
What elements of character from this genre am I inspired by?			

2 From your reading in this unit, what characters could inspire the creation of your own character? Write down your ideas about how you may modify an existing character from one of the genres you have read, or how you may be inspired by the qualities of this character.

3 What are the qualities and main values of your protagonist?

Common to the genres of gothic fiction, fantasy and fairy tale is a character who needs to overcome a challenge or needs to learn something important about themselves. This helps readers build a relationship with the character and learn important life lessons, too.

Read the following extract from Harry Potter and the Philosopher's Stone *by J.K. Rowling. Harry has arrived at Hogwarts School of Witchcraft and Wizardry after only recently learning that he is a wizard, and he is about to be sorted into his house group. This is an uncomfortable moment for Harry and one of the first tests of his character.*

Harry Potter and the Philosopher's Stone

by J.K. Rowling

'I shall return when we are ready for you,' said Professor McGonagall. 'Please wait quietly.'

She left the chamber. Harry swallowed.

'How exactly do they sort us into houses?' he asked Ron.

'Some sort of test, I think. Fred said it hurts a lot, but I think he was joking.'

Harry's heart gave a horrible jolt. A test? In front of the whole school? But he didn't know any magic yet – what on earth would he have to do? He hadn't expected something like this the moment they arrived. He looked around anxiously and saw that everyone else looked terrified too. No one was talking much except Hermione Granger, who was whispering very fast about all the spells she'd learnt and wondering which one she'd need. Harry tried hard not to listen to her. He'd never been more nervous, never, not even when he'd had to take a school report home to the Dursleys saying that he'd somehow turned his teacher's wig blue. He kept his eyes fixed on the door. Any second now, Professor McGonagall would come back and lead him to his doom.

INTERPRET

Discuss with a partner why two short sentences are used here.

INTERPRET

Discuss with a partner why repeated questions are used in this section.

INTERPRET

What choices has the writer made in this text to reveal Harry's character? Discuss with a partner.

1.3.4 Expressing ideas and composing texts A

Position your character in a moment of challenge or a situation in which they must face an obstacle. Write about this experience.

Your goal is to create a clear character voice that reveals the character's main values.

- Choose either first person or third person **point of view**.
- Use characteristics from a combination of genres to create your character.
- Vary your sentences to mirror the character's state of mind.

VOCABULARY

point of view
noun: the position from which the subject matter of a text is viewed. The creator of the text controls what we see and how we relate to the situation, character and ideas.

How can I combine genres to create setting and atmosphere in my own text?

You will need to make decisions about the setting of your imaginative appropriation. Setting refers to the physical place and time in which the events of the story happen. Setting is important in creating **atmosphere** for your text and helping readers understand your intended message or purpose. Your choice of setting should also reflect something about your character. Why are they here? How will an experience in this place impact their values and beliefs?

VOCABULARY

atmosphere
noun: the feeling or sense created by a setting or place that contributes to the overall mood of the story.

In the next part of this chapter, you will make decisions about the setting of your imaginative text and carefully consider how you can use vocabulary, syntax and figurative language to create atmosphere for your readers.

1.3.5 Expressing ideas and composing texts A

1 Return to Chapter 1 and revise the typical settings of each genre. Consider how you can be inspired by these settings and complete the table below to begin planning your setting.

	Gothic fiction	Fantasy	Fairy tale
What elements of setting from this genre am I inspired by?			

2 From your reading in this unit, what settings could inspire the creation of your own setting? Write down your ideas about how you may modify an existing setting from one of the genres you have read, or how you may be inspired by the qualities of this setting.

____

____

____

____

3 Describe the setting for your text. What kind of atmosphere do you want to create in this setting?

____

____

____

____

Writers make deliberate decisions in **syntax** and **vocabulary** to create atmosphere in their texts. This may include decisions about the structure and types of sentences used and the selection of words used. Together, these elements create a feeling for readers about the setting.

VOCABULARY

syntax
noun: refers to the arrangement of words to create phrases and sentences. There are basic rules for syntax, including the need for every sentence to have a subject and a verb. Another rule is the correct use of tense (past, present or future).

vocabulary
noun: refers to a collection of words, selected to create particular effects on the reader.

Writers may also use **imagery** and **figurative language** to create atmosphere in a setting. Both forms of language help readers visualise the setting and begin to associate feelings with the physical location.

Read the following extract from The Woman in Black by Susan Hill. Here, the narrator is awoken by strange sounds and leaves her room to investigate.

VOCABULARY

imagery
noun: occurs when words are used to help readers create a mental image of what is being described, often by activating the senses.

figurative language
noun: refers to using words and phrases to mean something other than their literal meaning. This could be achieved through devices such as metaphor, simile, personification or symbolism.

The Woman in Black

by Susan Hill

... Then from somewhere, out of that howling darkness, a cry came to my ears, catapulting me back into the present and banishing all tranquillity.

I listened hard. Nothing. The tumult of the wind, like a banshee, and the banging and rattling of the window in its old, ill-fitting frame. Then yes, again, a cry, that familiar cry of desperation and anguish, a cry for help from a child somewhere out on the marsh.

There was no child. I knew that. How could there be? Yet how could I lie here and ignore even the crying of some long-dead ghost?

... As I ventured down the landing towards the stairs, Spider the dog followed me at once, two things happened together. I had the impression of someone who had just that very second before gone past me on their way from the top of the stairs to one of the other rooms, and, as a tremendous blast of wind hit the house so that it all but seemed to rock at the impact, the lights went out.

INTERPRET

Underline examples of figurative language used in the text.

INTERPRET

Circle vocabulary that you think contributes to the atmosphere of this extract.

INTERPRET

What syntax choices has the writer made to create atmosphere? Discuss with a partner.

1.3.6 Expressing ideas and composing texts A

Position your character in a particular part of the story's setting. Write about this experience. Your goal is to create an atmosphere that engages readers in the setting.

- Carefully consider the selection of words (vocabulary).
- Use figurative language and imagery to create atmosphere.
- Vary the syntax of your sentences to engage readers.

1.3.7 Chapter reflection

1 In groups of four, share and discuss your writing from this chapter. Discuss what you like about each other's characters and settings and also what could be improved.

2 What writing experiences did you enjoy in this chapter?

3 What writing experiences did you find challenging in this chapter?

4 Let's return to this unit's inquiry question: *How do narratives rework and combine elements of genre to create new, engaging texts?* How have your learning and reading experiences in chapter 3 addressed the inquiry question?

Unit 1: **Summative assessment**

The summative assessment options below provide opportunities to demonstrate your achievement of the following outcomes and content points.

Outcome and focus area	EN4-RVL-01 Reading, viewing and listening to texts	EN4-URA-01 Understanding and responding to texts A	EN4-URB-01 Understanding and responding to texts B	EN4-URC-01 Understanding and responding to texts C	EN4-ECA-01 Expressing ideas and composing texts A
Content point	Reading for challenge, interest and enjoyment	Narrative	Style	Genre Intertextuality	Text features: imaginative Sentence-level grammar and punctuation Word-level language

Option 1:

Write your own **appropriation** of a well-known narrative that combines elements of the gothic fiction, fantasy and fairy tale genres. Your imaginative piece is to be written for a contemporary, modern audience.

Ensure that your response:
- combines elements of **genre** to create a new, refreshed text
- experiments with a range of **narrative** structural elements to engage readers
- **transforms** and **appropriates** aspects of well-known texts in your own personal style
- controls and experiments with aspects of **syntax**, **vocabulary**, **imagery** and **figurative language** to create meaning.

Option 2:

Recreate a text examined in this unit in another mode or a combination of multiple modes.

For example, write the narrative version of a film scene, or create a graphic novel version of a narrative.

Ensure that your response:
- combines elements of **genre** to create a new, refreshed text
- experiments with a range of **narrative** structural elements to engage readers
- **transforms** and **appropriates** aspects of well-known texts in your own personal style
- controls and experiments with aspects of **syntax**, **vocabulary**, **imagery** and **figurative language** to create meaning.

Option 3:

Transform a traditional, cultural folk tale into a modern narrative piece that uses elements of gothic fiction or fantasy.

Ensure that your response:

- combines elements of **genre** to create a new, refreshed text
- experiments with a range of **narrative** structural elements to engage readers
- **transforms** and **appropriates** aspects of well-known texts in your own personal style
- controls and experiments with aspects of **syntax**, **vocabulary**, **imagery** and **figurative language** to create meaning.

Assessment as learning: self-assessment

Does my response:

- ☐ demonstrate an understanding of genre?
- ☐ use a range of narrative structural elements in unexpected and new ways?
- ☐ maintain a personal writing style inspired by writers examined in this unit?
- ☐ demonstrate control of syntax, vocabulary, imagery and figurative language?

What are two strengths of my response?

____

____

What area/s of my response do I need to refine further?

____

____

____

____

UNIT 02

Against all odds

Unit inquiry question:
How do texts reflect the individual and shared experience of fortitude and resilience?

In this unit, students will engage with a range of texts that reflect experiences of adversity and challenge. They will analyse how themes of fortitude, resilience and perseverance are represented, deepening their reading, viewing and listening skills across a range of modes. They will closely examine how point of view and characterisation are crafted in texts to reflect varied individual and shared responses to adversity. Students will compose analytical and informative responses that demonstrate an appreciation of the ways texts inspire audiences to persevere, both individually and collectively, in times of challenge.

To address the focus inquiry question of the unit, students will engage with learning in three chapters:

CHAPTER 4

Responding to adversity

In this chapter, students will examine how texts reflect different types and experiences of adversity. They will consider how people may respond to adversity with resilience and courage, as represented in texts across multiple modes, including poetry. They will be introduced to how point of view is established to engage audiences.

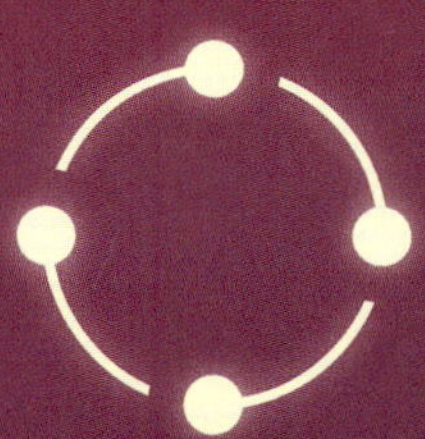

CHAPTER 5

Personal perseverance

In this chapter, students will examine how experiences of adversity can impact an individual's identity and how personal fortitude and perseverance can result in growth and development. To exemplify this, students will examine characterisation and point of view in the film *Lion* directed by Garth Davis.

CHAPTER 6

Strength in numbers

In this final chapter, students will continue their exploration of characterisation and point of view to examine how texts reflect shared experiences of fortitude. They will consider how texts can inspire people to unite for the common, greater good.

The learning activities within each chapter and the summative assessment options (on pages 80-81) provide opportunities to assess student achievement of the following outcomes and content points.

Outcome and focus area	Content point
EN4-RVL-01 **Reading, viewing and listening to texts**	**Reading, viewing and listening skills** Use contextual cues to infer the meaning of unfamiliar words Apply a range of strategies to develop fluency in reading aloud, including an understanding of pace, tone and voice Revisit texts to develop a clear understanding of the themes, ideas and attitudes they express
EN4-URA-01 **Understanding and responding to texts A**	**Point of view** Recognise how texts engage and position the audience to perceive events, characters and ideas using narrative voice and focalisers, tense, sequencing and intrusion, and apply this understanding in own texts Understand how choice of first, second and third-person voice can establish different relationships between creator and audience, and experiment with changes in point of view in own texts **Characterisation** Analyse how engaging characters are constructed in texts through a range of language features and structures, and use these features and structures in own texts Describe how characters in texts, including stereotypes, archetypes, flat and rounded, static and dynamic characters represent values and attitudes, and experiment with these in own texts Understand how the interactions of characters, such as protagonists and antagonists, might be perceived to represent aspects of human relationships, and experiment with interactions when composing texts
EN4-URB-01 **Understanding and responding to texts B**	**Theme** Understand how repetition, patterning and language features used within a text communicate ideas about social, personal, ethical and philosophical issues and experiences, and demonstrate this understanding through written, spoken, visual and multimodal responses

EN4-ECA-01	Writing
Expressing ideas and composing texts A	Apply understanding of the structural and grammatical codes and conventions of writing to shape meaning when composing imaginative, informative and analytical, and persuasive written texts Demonstrate control of structural and grammatical components to produce texts that are appropriate to topic, purpose and audience Understand the interconnectedness of textual features for the overall cohesive effect
	Text features: informative and analytical
	Compose texts that include a detailed introduction of ideas, the logical progression of supporting points, and a rhetorically effective conclusion, which reflect a broadening understanding of facts, concepts and perspectives beyond immediate experience Embed textual evidence within sentences to support the articulation of a personal perspective of a text Compose informative texts that summarise conceptual information Discuss a central idea, from personal and objective positions, to broaden the exploration of a concept

CHAPTER 4: RESPONDING TO ADVERSITY

Chapter overview

In this chapter, you will examine how texts reflect different types and experiences of adversity. You will consider how people may respond to adversity with resilience and courage. You will explore representations of adversity in various types of text including poetry, and be introduced to how point of view is established to engage audiences.

Success criteria: in this chapter, I will be successful when I can ...

- identify experiences of adversity represented in texts
- explain the differing ways people may respond to adversity by reading, viewing and listening to texts
- analyse the way resilience and courage are represented in texts as ways of responding to adversity
- compose texts from various points of view that reflect responses to adversity.

Chapter inquiry questions

- What are some types of adversity people may experience?
- How do some people respond to experiences of adversity?

Key vocabulary

- adversity
- point of view
- fortitude
- resilience
- courage

What are some types of adversity people may experience?

Adversity refers to a challenging period of difficulty, struggle or suffering. Unfortunately, many people experience adversity in their everyday lives. Some people may experience periods of adversity that are overcome, but there may also be periods of extended or unresolved adversity for many others. People may need the help of others to overcome adversity, or may need to find ways of living with adversity individually.

2.4.1 Warm-up

A time of personal challenge

Write about a time when you have been challenged or needed to overcome something difficult.

Remember, it's okay that your interpretations of 'challenge' are different from those of other people. What is challenging for one person may not be for another. Your experience is personal to you.

There are several causes and types of adversity that people may encounter in life. The following are some examples.

Physical adversity	Social adversity
A person may be restrained in their physical ability. For example, they may have an injury to the body or an ongoing disability. Another dimension to physical adversity may be aspects of the physical world that are providing hardship for a person – for example, a natural disaster or an aspect of climate.	On one level, social adversity may refer to a limited ability to communicate with others or maintain relationships. However, it may also refer to aspects of society that may present a challenge for some people – for example, gender stereotypes, political oppression or racism.
Financial adversity	**Mental/emotional adversity**
This type of adversity refers to economic hardship, or not having the financial means to obtain necessities such as food and shelter. Unfortunately, this is an increasingly common experience of hardship in our world that contributes to poverty, homelessness, decreased rates of education and a lack of access to healthcare.	Mental and emotional adversity refers to challenges people may face in regulating their emotions, and mental struggles such as depression, anxiety and other mental illnesses. This form of adversity may be linked to personal trauma or other aspects of a person's context.

2.4.2 Reading, viewing and listening to texts

1 **Find and watch each of the film trailers below online. What types of adversity are reflected in each of the films?**

Film	What types of adversity are reflected in the film?
The Boy Who Harnessed the Wind (2019)	
Ride Like a Girl (2019)	
The Impossible (2012)	

2 What is another text you have engaged with recently that reflects an experience of adversity? Explain what types of adversity are seen in that text.

Literature can be powerful in representing experiences of adversity and the different ways that people may respond to adversity. Readers can form a relationship with the creator of a text and respond to a text personally. They may develop empathy for the experience shared, inspire others to grow more aware of the adversities of others, or even become agents of change for a better world for all.

One way in which texts build this relationship between creator and audience is through **point of view**. In a narrative, this may be achieved through first, second or third person point of view. In films, images are positioned or arranged in a way that guides us to a position. In poetry or non-fiction texts, imagery, figurative language and rhetorical devices may be used to create point of view.

It is important to remember that point of view is controlled by the creator of a text, therefore certain information, values or beliefs are privileged. This means that we are manipulated to see what the text creator wants us to see, and often we adopt the same view.

DISCUSS

In groups, research first, second and third person point of view in narrative writing. Discuss the purpose of each point of view and find examples from texts you have read to support your ideas.

VOCABULARY

point of view
noun: the position from which the subject matter of a text is viewed. The creator of the text controls what we see and how we relate to the situation, character and ideas.

Read the extract from *Turtles All the Way Down* by John Green. Consider how point of view is used to reflect the adversity experienced by the narrator.

Turtles All the Way Down

by John Green

Hundreds of voices were shouting over one another in the cafeteria, so that the conversation became mere sound, the rushing of a river over rocks ... I was eating a peanut butter and honey sandwich and drinking a Dr Pepper. To be honest, I find the whole process of masticating plants and animals and then shoving them down my esophagus kind of disgusting, so I was trying not to think about the fact that I was eating, which is a form of thinking about it.

... I felt my stomach begin to work on the sandwich, and even over everybody's talking, I could hear it digesting, all the bacteria chewing the slime of peanut butter – the students inside of me eating at my internal cafeteria. A shiver convulsed through me.

'Didn't you go to camp with him?' Daisy asked me.

'With who?'

'Davis Pickett,' she said.

'Yeah,' I said. 'Why?'

'Aren't you listening?' Daisy asked. I am listening, I thought, to the cacophony of my digestive tract. Of course I'd long known that I was playing host to a massive collection of parasitic organisms, but I didn't much like being reminded of it. By cell count, humans are approximately 50 percent microbial, meaning that about half of the cells that make you up are not yours at all. There are something like a thousand times more microbes living in my particular biome than there are human beings on earth, and it often seems like I can feel them living and breeding and dying in and on me. I wiped my sweaty palms on my jeans and tried to control my breathing. Admittedly, I have some anxiety problems, but I would argue it isn't irrational to be concerned about the fact that you are a skin-encased bacterial colony.

INTERPRET

Identify and label the narrative point of view used in this extract.

INTERPRET

Circle examples of the character's experience of adversity.

2.4.3 Understanding and responding to texts A

1 Explain the experience of adversity represented in this text. Refer to textual evidence to support your answer.

2 How does the chosen point of view create a relationship between the narrator and the reader? Refer to textual evidence to support your answer.

____

____

____

____

3 Research other young adult fiction texts that also reflect this type of adversity. Discuss your research with your peers.

How do some people respond to experiences of adversity?

Responses to adversity are widely varied. The path to overcoming or living with adversity is not straightforward. Again, literature is powerful in helping us to understand varied responses to adversity and consider our role in helping others with their challenges.

One approach that some take in living with adversity is having **fortitude** and **resilience**.

DISCUSS

In groups, discuss your understanding of **fortitude** and **resilience.** Where have you heard these words before? What do they mean? What examples can you give of fortitude and resilience from your life?

For many centuries, poetry has been a powerful vehicle for sharing experiences of resilience in the face of adversity. Two significant poems that do this are 'Invictus' by William Ernest Henley and 'Still I Rise' by Maya Angelou. Let's compare the way the two poets respond to adversity.

DISCUSS

Research the context of each poem before you read them below. What experience of adversity was faced by each poet?

Invictus

by William Ernest Henley

Out of the night that covers me,
Black as the pit from pole to pole,
I thank whatever gods may be
For my unconquerable soul.

In the fell clutch of circumstance
I have not winced nor cried aloud.
Under the bludgeonings of chance
My head is bloody, but unbowed.

Beyond this place of wrath and tears
Looms but the Horror of the shade,
And yet the menace of the years
Finds and shall find me unafraid.

It matters not how strait the gate,
How charged with punishments the scroll,
I am the master of my fate,
I am the captain of my soul.

Still I Rise

by Maya Angelou

You may write me down in history
With your bitter, twisted lies,
You may trod me in the very dirt
But still, like dust, I'll rise.
...
Did you want to see me broken?
Bowed head and lowered eyes?
Shoulders falling down like teardrops,
Weakened by my soulful cries?
...
You may shoot me with your words,
You may cut me with your eyes,
You may kill me with your hatefulness,
But still, like air, I'll rise.
...
Leaving behind nights of terror and fear
I rise
Into a daybreak that's wondrously clear
I rise
Bringing the gifts that my ancestors gave,
I am the dream and the hope of the slave.
I rise
I rise
I rise.

2.4.4 Understanding and responding to texts A

1 What is similar about the two poets' approaches to adversity?

2 Select a significant quotation from each poem that you feel best reflects the poet's point of view. Explain why you chose this quotation and how it builds a relationship with the reader.

Quotation (remember to use quotation marks)	Explanation
Invictus	
Still I Rise	

3 **Explain how both the poets use both negative and positive imagery to show the contrast between their circumstances and their attitudes towards adversity. Refer to textual evidence to support your answer.**

To face adversity, no matter the size or scale, takes **courage**. Some people may be forced to overcome adversity alone, while others may have a great support network around them. Either way, every small step towards living with adversity or challenging the causes of adversity requires courage.

Read the poem The Battle *by Tara Finn.*

The Battle

by Tara Finn

Defenceless I stand,
Before the enemy,
I am courage,
My opponent; fear,
Both strong,
But opposite,
A fight to overcome,
A fear,
Strong I stand,
Ready for battle.

2.4.5 Expressing ideas and composing texts A

1 Choose one text you have engaged with in this chapter. Create a visual representation of the battle between the character and their experience of adversity, inspired by Tara Finn's poem.

2 Tara Finn's poem personifies fear as an opponent. This means that she makes fear almost like a person that she will battle. Write a brief imaginative piece that personifies an experience of adversity for either you or a character in a text you have engaged with in this chapter.

2.4.6 Chapter reflection

1 Summarise your understanding of the term 'adversity'.

2 What have you learned about the ways that people may respond to adversity?

3 Let's return to this unit's inquiry question: ***How do texts reflect the individual and shared experience of fortitude and resilience?*** How have your learning and reading experiences in chapter 4 addressed the inquiry question?

CHAPTER 5: PERSONAL PERSEVERANCE

Chapter overview

In this chapter, you will investigate the ways in which film can represent personal experiences of adversity through close examination of *Lion* (2016) directed by Garth Davis. You will focus on the way film features are used to craft point of view and characterisation, enabling audiences to appreciate how personal fortitude and perseverance can result in a stronger sense of identity. You will compose analytical responses that demonstrate your understanding of these processes and your developing personal perspectives.

Success criteria: in this chapter, I will be successful when I can ...

- identify film features that are used to reflect personal experiences of adversity
- explain how point of view and characterisation are created through film features
- analyse how film represents the renewed sense of identity that can result from personal fortitude
- compose analytical responses that demonstrate personal perspectives supported by textual evidence.

Chapter inquiry questions

- How can film represent personal experiences of adversity?
- How can film represent personal perseverance as a way of responding to adversity?
- How can personal fortitude contribute to a renewed sense of identity?

Key vocabulary

- point of view
- characterisation
- camera shots
- sound
- editing
- perseverance
- dynamic character
- identity
- theme

How can film represent personal experiences of adversity?

Film is a powerful medium in representing experiences of adversity, as audiences become immersed in the character's life and the events of the film. In this chapter, you will closely examine the representation of adversity and fortitude in the 2016 film *Lion* directed by Garth Davis. You will investigate how the director creates **point of view** through film features and builds **characterisation** so that we become emotionally invested in Saroo's story.

2.5.1 Warm-up

What does your world look like from above?

The film *Lion* is based on the true story of Saroo Brierley, who at the age of five was separated from his family in India, becoming lost after falling asleep on a train which took him approximately 1,500 km from home. He was later adopted by a family in Australia, yet always yearned to find his home. Not knowing the name of his hometown, Saroo spent three years of his life searching for it using Google Earth and his memory. After 25 years, Saroo found his way home and was reunited with his family.

What does your immediate world look like from above? Use Google Earth and look around your neighbourhood. Can you see familiar landmarks? Can you trace your way home from another location using only memory?

2.5.2 Reading, viewing and listening to texts

Find the film trailer for the movie Lion *online and watch it.*

1 Explain two types of adversity reflected in the film.

2 What have you learned about Saroo's character from the trailer?

3 Describe the point of view that is created in this trailer.

We are positioned to view Saroo's adversity from his perspective by being aligned with his **point of view.** The first section of the film positions us to see Saroo's adversity as a young child, living in the context of poverty and with a lack of education. However, despite this adversity, we are also positioned to see the love shared between Saroo and his family – particularly his mother and his brother, Guddu. As an audience, we understand that this love, together with Saroo's determination to work hard and contribute to the family even at such a young age, helps him live with the adversities of his context. This point of view positions us to see Saroo's characteristics of perseverance and fortitude, which we know will shape him as an adult.

Filmmakers and directors use the features of film to create and maintain point of view. Let's refresh your knowledge of some of these features. Explain how you think each of these features contributes to the way point of view is created.

Camera shots	Description	How do you think this contributes to point of view?
Medium shot	Shows one or more characters from the waist up engaging together	
Wide shot	Shows the entire character and how they are positioned in relation to their surroundings	
Point of view	Shows the audience what a character sees with the camera acting like that character's eyes	
Close-up	Shows the character from the shoulders up, usually focused on facial expression	

Sound	Description	How do you think this contributes to point of view?
Voiceover	A recording of a character's voice added to a section of the film	
Music	Music added to the film that mirrors the emotional intensity of the scene	

Editing	Description	How do you think this contributes to point of view?
Montage	The arrangement of a series of short clips added together to create a longer sequence	
Motif	A recurring image, symbol, visual feature or sound that represents a deeper theme or idea	

2.5.3 Understanding and responding to texts A

Find the opening scene of *Lion* online and watch how it shows life in his village before he was lost.

1 Identify and explain how one **camera shot** has been used to position us to see the enormity of the Indian landscape. Why is this set up at the beginning of the film?

2 Saroo is shown to engage with a butterfly in this scene, and images of butterflies recur throughout the film. What could this motif suggest about Saroo's character?

3 What film features are used to show the relationship between Saroo and Guddu?

The greatest adversity Saroo faces is becoming lost on the train and subsequently being unable to find his way home. The representation of the moment he wakes on the moving train and discovers he is trapped is particularly harrowing, as we are positioned through point of view to feel his terror and panic.

INTERPRET

Journal your feelings as you watch this scene. What film features do you think are contributing to the way you feel?

Find and watch the 'train scene' from the film online.

2.5.4 Expressing ideas and composing texts A

How are film features used in the 'train scene' to reflect Saroo's experience of adversity?

- Write an analytical paragraph to respond to this question.
- Identify Saroo's experience of adversity in your topic sentence.
- Explain how at least two film features are used to show his experience in this scene.
- Refer to specific textual evidence from the scene to support your discussion of film features.
- Discuss the way viewers are positioned to feel in this scene and what we learn about Saroo's character.

How can film represent personal perseverance as a way of responding to adversity?

As discussed in chapter 4, there are many ways of responding to adversity. *Lion* shows that Saroo responds to his adversity with personal perseverance.

DISCUSS

Discuss with a partner your understanding of the word **perseverance**. Where have you heard this word before? What are some examples of how people may persevere through hardship?

Although the character of Saroo is based on a real person, the filmmakers have used elements of **characterisation** to engage audiences in his personal journey. Saroo is presented as an engaging character and one who is **dynamic**, meaning that he changes and grows as the film progresses.

When we first see Saroo, as an adult who has moved from Hobart to Melbourne to undertake study at a private college, we understand that he feels conflicted about his heritage and past. When he is asked about his background, he makes jokes to distract from the pain associated with his past. We also see that he feels disconnected from his Indian heritage, despite his adoptive parents remaining open and transparent about this aspect of his life.

A turning point in his attitude towards his past comes when he attends a dinner at the house of his Indian–Australian friends. Memories of his past are triggered when he sees and tastes an Indian dessert.

Find the 'I'm Lost' scene from the film online and watch it.

2.5.5 Understanding and responding to texts A

1 What do you learn about Saroo's character in this scene?

2 How do sound and editing features in this scene position Saroo's point of view? Refer to textual evidence.

3 What is significant about Saroo's final line of dialogue, 'I'm not from Calcutta. I'm lost'?

The film's title comes from the Hindi meaning of Saroo's birth name, Sheru. As an adult, Saroo discovers that he pronounced his name wrongly when he was lost and searching for his family. The image of a lion is often associated with strength and courage. This seems particularly fitting for Saroo as he needs to draw on all his strength to persevere in his extreme adversity.

When Saroo decides to search for his home using the (at this time) relatively new software Google Earth, he is guided by only his memories from childhood. The film shows that Saroo becomes consumed by his search and starts to lose contact with his adoptive family and close friends.

2.5.6 Understanding and responding to texts A

1 Examine the screenshot showing Saroo recording his search on a map.

2 In small groups, brainstorm words that relate to the values that Saroo's character reflects about responding to adversity.

3 Write these words around the image.

We see that Saroo's perseverance and dedication pay off late one night when he finds a location from his memory on Google Earth. This leads him to find the name of his village and his family's home on the map, after three years of searching. This is a particularly emotional scene, which skilfully edits Saroo's memories together with his online search.

Find the 'memory/Google Earth scene' from the film online and watch it.

2.5.7 Understanding and responding to texts A

1 Identify examples of the following film features used in this scene and explain how they emotionally impact the audience.

Film feature	Example	How does this emotionally impact the audience?
Sound – silence		
Sound – music		
Camera shot – close-up		
Editing		

2 **What does this scene suggest about Saroo's character and the way he has responded to adversity?**

It is nearly time to compose a personal response to Saroo's characterisation. But first, take some time to talk about the following discussion points with a small group:

- What does the director want us to appreciate about Saroo's response to adversity?
- What values does Saroo's character represent?
- Do you think Saroo's response and ways of overcoming adversity are 'the norm'? Is the story realistic?
- Why do you think it is important for the audience to build an emotional connection with Saroo?
- What moment in the film emotionally impacted you?

2.5.8 Expressing ideas and composing texts A

How effective do you think the characterisation of Saroo is in revealing ways of responding to adversity?

- Write an analytical paragraph to respond to this question.
- Outline a position regarding the effectiveness of characterisation in your topic sentence.
- Identify one or two key scenes that support this position and explain how film features are used to craft characterisation.
- Refer to specific textual evidence to support your discussion of film features.
- Discuss the way viewers are positioned to respond to Saroo's character and the values he represents.

How can personal fortitude contribute to a renewed sense of identity?

Saroo's fortitude not only results in him finding his home and family but also contributes to a stronger, more certain sense of **identity**. Although he was happy with his Australian adopted family and he assures them that they will always be his parents, his desire to reconnect with his mother is constant and unwavering.

> **VOCABULARY**
>
> **theme**
> *noun:* may be seen simply as the message or moral of a story or text. A theme may also be described as a writer's attitude or belief about a certain topic, presented as a statement about life.

Another of the film's most significant **themes** is love. Love is present in many ways in the film: the love between mother and son; brotherly love (both Saroo's everlasting bond with Guddu and his conflicted love with Mantosh, his adopted brother); and a new, steadfast and accepting love with Lucy.

Examine these screenshots of moments of love from the film and then complete the activity. The first screenshot shows Saroo as a child with his adopted mum, Sue. The second shows his reunion as an adult with his birth mother at the end of the film.

2.5.9 Understanding and responding to texts A

1 What is shown about the theme of love in each of the screenshot images?

____

____

____

2 Explain how another part of the film reflects an aspect of love.

____

____

____

3 What overall idea do you think the film reflects about the theme of love in relation to adversity?

____

____

____

The theme of love is also expressed in the film's final scene as Saroo, as an adult, walks along the train tracks while visualising his younger self and his brother Guddu. This comes after Saroo learns that Guddu was killed on the night that Saroo got lost on the train.

This final scene also reflects identity as another key theme of the film. Although he faced the physical adversity of losing his home and family, Saroo was also challenged by a lack of identity. He felt conflicted in his cultural identity between his Australian and Indian heritage. In his personal identity, he was torn between his adopted family and his birth family. However, the ending of the film shows that he finds a renewed identity, learning to accept all these parts of himself.

Find the 'ending scene' of the film online and watch it.

2.5.10 Expressing ideas and composing texts A

How does the **motif** of train tracks shown in the final scene of the film reflect the renewed direction that Saroo gained from his adversity?

- Write an analytical paragraph to respond to this question.
- Outline an idea about what the motif reflects about Saroo's character in your topic sentence.
- Explain how film features are used in the scene to reflect Saroo's renewed direction and identity.
- Refer to specific textual evidence to support your discussion of film features.
- Discuss the way viewers are positioned to respond to Saroo's character and the values he represents.

2.5.11 Chapter reflection

1 What have you learned about the way this film represents personal adversity?

2 What new knowledge did you gain about the way film features position audiences to see character and point of view?

3 Let's return to this unit's inquiry question: ***How do texts reflect the individual and shared experience of fortitude and resilience?*** How have your learning and reading experiences in chapter 5 addressed the inquiry question?

CHAPTER 6: STRENGTH IN NUMBERS

Chapter overview

In this final chapter of the unit, you will continue your exploration of characterisation and point of view to examine how texts reflect shared experiences of fortitude. You will look closely at how people can inspire others by challenging assumptions and expectations, and how texts can inspire people to work together to create change and overcome adversity. You will also compose responses that share your personal perspective on this topic, supported by discussions of texts examined in the unit.

Success criteria: In this chapter, I will be successful when I can ...

- describe how point of view and characterisation are crafted differently in fiction and non-fiction texts
- explain how texts challenge assumptions and expectations
- analyse how texts use language to inspire others to change and overcome adversity together
- compose analytical responses that demonstrate personal perspectives supported by textual evidence.

Chapter inquiry questions

- How can people challenge stereotypes and assumptions?
- How can one person's fortitude inspire others?
- How can we work together to create change and overcome adversity?

Key vocabulary

- stereotypes
- assumptions
- call to action
- rhetoric
- ethos
- logos
- pathos

How can people challenge stereotypes and assumptions?

One form of social adversity is when people feel restricted or limited by **stereotypes** and **assumptions**. A stereotype is a widely held or generalised idea about a person or group of people. In a similar way, an assumption is a belief that a person has about an idea that has not been tested or proven. Stereotypes and assumptions are often caused by inequalities in society, ideas passed on from family members or friends, an unwillingness to understand other people's experiences, or not spending time with people who have different ways of living or seeing the world.

2.6.1 Warm-up

Who is a person who inspires you?

Write about an inspirational person. This could be a person in your life, a historical or well-known figure, a fictional character or a person from a time long ago. What makes this person inspiring?

DISCUSS

In a group of four or five students, discuss the following questions.

- What are some commonly known stereotypes or assumptions?
- Why are these stereotypes or assumptions damaging?
- How can stereotypes and assumptions create adversity?
- How do you think we can move beyond these stereotypes and assumptions?

One way in which we can move beyond stereotypes and assumptions is by educating ourselves about the different ways people live and think. We can do this by reading about the experiences of others or listening to their stories. We will now examine how some texts that challenge stereotypes and assumptions.

Read the following extract from *The War That Saved My Life* by Kimberly Brubaker Bradley. The novel tells the story of ten-year-old Ada who was born with a club foot and has never been allowed to leave her apartment. However, when World War II breaks out, Ada escapes with her brother Jamie who is being evacuated to the country. There, in a loving foster home, she learns to walk, run and ride a horse. This extract shares her experience after helping to catch a German spy.

The War That Saved My Life

by Kimberly Brubaker Bradley

The army had found the suitcase buried in the sand. It contained a radio transmitter, the sort spies used to send coded messages across the channel. The perfect Englishman really *had* been a spy.

I became a hero. The RAF men at the airfield bought me chocolate; the WVS women pooled together a tablespoon of sugar each, and gave me a whole bag. Daisy's mother from the pub hugged me whenever she saw me, and every time I went into the village I was greeted with smiles and shouts of, 'There's our little spy-catcher!' or 'There's our good lass!'

It was as if I'd been born in the village. As if I'd been born with two strong feet. As if I really was someone important, someone loved.

Jamie made me repeat the story over and over again. 'Tell me,' he'd beg. 'Tell me your hero story.'

... *Hero* wasn't a word I was used to hearing. The admiration was interesting, but the attention made me feel unsettled.

'Say it again,' Jamie said, giggling. 'Tell me what you told the first [police] officer.'

'He looked at my bad foot,' I said, 'and I said, "my foot's a long way from my brain."'

INTERPRET

Underline any words you are unfamiliar with and discuss with a partner the clues in the text that help you understand these words.

INTERPRET

Circle examples that show that stereotypes or assumptions have been challenged.

2.6.2 Understanding and responding to texts A

1 What have you learned about Ada's character from this extract?

______

______

2 Identify one stereotype or assumption presented in the text. How does Ada challenge this stereotype or assumption?

______

______

______

3 How is Ada's point of view about adversity reflected in this extract?

Reading about how people challenge stereotypes and assumptions can be very inspiring. Texts might even use a **call to action** when representing themes of adversity to inspire others to be part of a solution.

Read the following extract from Maxine Beneba Clarke's poem 'Climate March Chant (a poem for many voices)' and then complete the activity below.

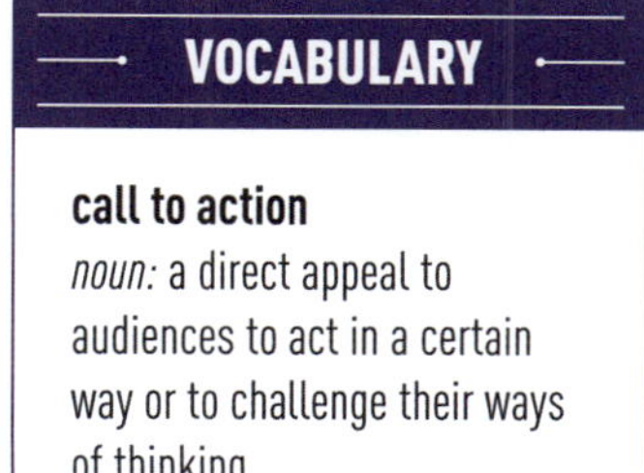

Climate March Chant (a poem for many voices)

by Maxine Beneba Clarke

Our voices might be tiny,
but our feet beat the drum:
a-thundering the streets
like *thump-a thump thump.*

Signs raised, fists raised,
rage raised high.
Holding cardboard placards
that we made last night.

We might not be grown-ups,
but we mean to save the world:
our way, any way,
we'll make the truth be heard.

Hurricane, tornado,
volcano, fire, flood.
We know some kids are starving,
cause the crops are drying up.

Our voices might be tiny,
but our feet beat the drum:
a-thundering the streets
like *thump-a thump thump.*

INTERPRET

Circle examples that show stereotypes or assumptions have been challenged.

LANGUAGE

Tick the following poetic features that have been used in this poem.

- ◯ metaphor
- ◯ onomatopoeia
- ◯ rhythm
- ◯ repetition
- ◯ inclusive language

2.6.3 Understanding and responding to texts B

1 What is reflected about the theme of adversity in the poem?

____

____

2 What stereotypes or assumptions does the poem challenge about children?

____

____

____

3 How is one form of poetic language used to create a call to action for readers?

____

____

____

Extension activity

In 2018, Australian school children walked out of school to protest about climate change. This event made national headlines across all forms of media.

Research some of the reporting about this event. What does this reflect about people coming together to face adversity? What assumptions about children and teenagers does it also challenge? With a partner, create a small presentation that shares your opinion on this topic.

How can one person's fortitude inspire others?

There is no doubt that stories of individual perseverance and fortitude are inspiring, and we often respond with 'warm and fuzzy' feelings when we hear of these experiences. Others may benefit from these stories by gaining more confidence to overcome their own adversity, or may help others to do the same.

In Australia, we are particularly fond of 'underdog' stories. An underdog may be a person who is thought to have little chance of winning a contest or coming out on top against a bigger, more powerful opponent. This person may have little status in society, may not be physically suited to a task, or may be assumed to be out of their depth with all the odds against them.

DISCUSS

Research some of the following underdog people and stories. What is inspiring about these stories?

Sport: Steven Bradbury, Lionel Rose, Eric Moussambani

Film: *Cool Runnings, The Castle, Eddie the Eagle*

Historical people: Vincent Lingiari, Emmeline Pankhurst, Buffalo Calf Road Woman

You will now read an extract from the novel *Runt* by Craig Silvey. In this story, Annie is an 11-year-old girl who lives in Upson Downs with her adopted stray dog called Runt. She is quirky and strives to always help others; she even wears a tool belt in case she ever needs to fix something. To win money to save her family's farm, Annie and Runt compete in a dog agility contest and become national champions without any training or preparation. Curiously, Runt only obeys Annie's commands when no one else is watching! They travel to London to compete in a prestigious dog show after the town raises funds for them. The extract shows that support for the unlikely duo is contagious in the town on the day of the competition.

Runt

by Craig Silvey

At Upson Downs Primary, students and staff and parents have gathered in the assembly hall to watch the Krumpets Dog Show on a projection screen. There are bright streamers and balloons and signs on the walls that say GO ANNIE! and COME ON RUNT!

As a school project, every student has knitted their own rainbow beanie and they wear them now. Some have taken their support a step further, digging through their own sheds at home to find tool belts as a tribute to Annie.

It warms the heart of Mrs Formsby, who wishes Annie were here to see it.

... It seems everyone in Upson Downs is watching.

There's an electricity in the air. A strange stillness. The kind of tension and excitement that makes the hair on the back of your neck stand up. A sense that something truly extraordinary is about to happen. And it is all because of Annie Shearer and Runt.

INTERPRET

The dog's name is Runt. Discuss the ideas associated with this name and how this positions him as an 'underdog'.

INTERPRET

Circle examples that show how Annie and Runt's fortitude inspires others.

INTERPRET

Discuss the metaphor of electricity in this final paragraph. What does this represent about Annie and Runt's impact on others?

2.6.4 Expressing ideas and composing texts A

How can one person's fortitude inspire others?

Write an analytical paragraph in response to this question, referring to the extract from *Runt* by Craig Silvey.

- Identify an idea in the text about fortitude inspiring others in your topic sentence.
- Describe how the characters in the text challenge stereotypes and assumptions.
- Explain how this idea is reflected in the text, drawing on specific textual evidence to support your discussion.
- Discuss the way readers are positioned to feel about the characters' impact on others.

How can we work together to create change and overcome adversity?

Stories of fortitude and perseverance can create social change, inspiring people to reduce adversity for others or work to find solutions for ongoing hardships. While one person may be instrumental in starting change, we know that we are more likely to achieve change when we work together. One of the first steps in creating change is awareness and collective support.

In 2023, the Australian women's football team, the Matildas, became the first Australian team ever to reach a semifinal in a football World Cup. The nation stood behind the team, and support for women's sport was at an all-time high. In fact, more people watched the Matildas' Round 16 match against Denmark than had watched the men's NRL or AFL grand finals in 2022. However, underlying this amazing show of collective support is the reality that women's sport is underfunded in comparison with men's sport in Australia, and that women across a range of sports do not receive the same pay as men.

Use the QR code to access and read 'From handing out their own flyers, to sell-out games: how the Matildas won over a nation', an article published by The Conversation.

DISCUSS

In small groups, discuss what you have read in this article. What social adversities are discussed? How might the collective support for the Matildas help create change in the world of sport?

A speech is a powerful medium for inspiring others to work together to create change and overcome adversity in our world. The art of using language persuasively to evoke a response in readers is called **rhetoric**. To appeal to their audience, speakers may rely on three forms of rhetorical appeal: **ethos**, **logos** and **pathos**.

To create these appeals, a range of rhetorical features may be used, including these.

Anecdote	Figurative language	Repetition
Sharing personal stories to exemplify an idea.	Using language that represents an idea in a non-literal way. For example, metaphor, simile, idiom, symbol, personification.	Repeating a key word or phrase multiple times.
Inclusive language	**Rhetorical questions**	**Rule of three**
Using pronouns that include the audience – we, us, our.	Asking questions and not expecting an answer.	Messages and words are remembered best in groups of three.

You will now examine extracts from two well-known speeches that aim to inspire audiences to work together to achieve change and overcome adversity. The first speech was given by Malala Yousafzai to the United Nations in 2013. The second speech was a poem delivered by Amanda Gorman at the 2021 inauguration of US President Joe Biden.

DISCUSS

Research the context of each speech. What experience of adversity was faced by each speaker?

Let's compare the way the two speeches use rhetoric to inspire audiences. After reading the speech extracts once, return to the texts and complete the following.

1 **Circle experiences of adversity.**

2 **Underline examples of rhetorical features used to inspire audiences.**

3 **Colour code examples of the three different types of rhetorical appeal: ethos, logos and pathos.**

United Nations Address

by Malala Yousafzai

So dear sisters and brothers, now it's time to speak up.
So today, we call upon the world leaders to change their strategic policies in favour of peace and prosperity. We call upon the world leaders that all the peace deals must protect women's and children's rights. A deal that goes against the rights of women is unacceptable.
We call upon all governments to ensure free compulsory education all over the world for every child.
We call upon all governments to fight against terrorism and violence, to protect children from brutality and harm.

The Hill We Climb

by Amanda Gorman

When day comes, we ask ourselves
where can we find light in this never-ending shade?
The loss we carry, a sea we must wade.
We've braved the belly of the beast.
We've learned that quiet isn't always peace,
and the norms and notions of what 'just is' isn't always 'justice'.
And yet, the dawn is ours before we knew it.
Somehow we do it.
Somehow we've weathered and witnessed a nation that isn't broken,
but simply unfinished.

... And yes, we are far from polished, far from pristine,
but that doesn't mean we are striving to form a union that is perfect.

... Dear brothers and sisters, we want schools and education for every child's bright future. We will continue our journey to our destination of peace and education. No one can stop us. We will speak for our rights and we will bring change through our voice. We believe in the power and the strength of our words. Our words can change the whole world.

... So let us wage a global struggle against illiteracy, poverty and terrorism. Let us pick up our books and our pens. They are our most powerful weapons. One child, one teacher, one book and one pen can change the world.

We are striving to forge our union with purpose.
To compose a country committed to all cultures, colors, characters, and conditions of man.
And so we lift our gazes not to what stands between us, but what stands before us.
We close the divide because we know, to put our future first, we must first put our differences aside.

... So let us leave behind a country better than the one we were left.
With every breath from my bronze-pounded chest, we will raise this wounded world into a wondrous one.
We will rise from the golden hills of the west.
We will rise from the wind-swept north-east where our forefathers first realized revolution.
We will rise from the lake-rimmed cities of the midwestern states.
We will rise from the sun-baked south.
We will rebuild, reconcile, and recover.
In every known nook of our nation, in every corner called our country,
our people, diverse and beautiful, will emerge, battered and beautiful.
When day comes, we step out of the shade, aflame and unafraid.
The new dawn blooms as we free it.
For there is always light,
if only we're brave enough to see it.
If only we're brave enough to be it.

2.6.5 Understanding and responding to texts B

1 What call to action does each speaker issue to their audience?

___

___

___

2 **Choose one of these speeches. How does the speaker use rhetoric to appeal to their audience? Refer to textual evidence to support your ideas.**

Now it is your turn to inspire others through rhetorical appeal.

2.6.6 Expressing ideas and composing texts A

Write the opening of a speech about a social adversity you are passionate about. Consider your call to action and what you hope to inspire others to aim to achieve.

- Identify the social adversity and the main idea you would like to convey about it.
- Use a range of rhetorical features to engage your audience.
- Choose a type (or types) of rhetorical appeal that you think will most effectively achieve your purpose.

2.6.7 Chapter reflection

1 What texts have you engaged with in this chapter that have inspired you in some way?

2 In what aspect of society do you think more change is needed to help others overcome adversity?

3 Let's return to this unit's inquiry question: ***How do texts reflect the individual and shared experience of fortitude and resilience?*** How have your learning and reading experiences in Chapter 6 addressed the inquiry question?

Unit 2: Summative assessment

The summative assessment options below provide opportunities to demonstrate your achievement of the following outcomes and content points.

Outcome and focus area	EN4-RVL-01 Reading, viewing and listening to texts	EN4-URA-01 Understanding and responding to texts A	EN4-URB-01 Understanding and responding to texts B	EN4-ECA-01 Expressing ideas and composing texts A
Content point	Reading, viewing and listening to texts	Point of view Characterisation	Theme	Writing Text features: informative and analytical

Option 1:

How have two texts examined in this unit explored how growth can be achieved from personal or shared fortitude?

Write an analytical response that discusses the representation of and responses to adversity in the texts, supported by discussion of language features.

Ensure that your response:

- outlines a main idea in response to the question
- develops ideas in a logically structured **analytical response**
- explains how **language** is used to reflect important **themes** about adversity
- provides a clear **point of view** expressed through purposeful language choices
- demonstrates **control of structure and language** to communicate personal perspectives.

Option 2:

There is always strength in numbers. If we work together, we can achieve greatness.

Write an extended analytical response that explains how *two* texts in this unit demonstrate the importance of working together to achieve social change. Consider how the texts use language to inspire audiences to act together or challenge ideas.

Ensure that your response:

- outlines a main idea in response to the question
- develops ideas in a logically structured **analytical response**
- explains how **language** is used to reflect important **themes** about adversity
- provides a clear **point of view** expressed through purposeful language choices
- demonstrates **control of structure and language** to communicate personal perspectives.

Option 3:

How have the point of view and characterisation in a text studied in this unit given you more understanding of fortitude and perseverance?

Write an analytical response that discusses the representation of and responses to adversity conveyed in one text, supported by discussion of language features.

Ensure that your response:

- outlines a main idea in response to the question
- develops ideas in a logically structured **analytical response**
- explains how **language** is used to reflect important themes about adversity
- provides a clear **point of view** expressed through purposeful language choices
- demonstrates **control of structure and language** to communicate personal perspectives.

Assessment as learning: self-assessment

Does my response:

- ☐ present a personal idea about adversity and fortitude?
- ☐ explain how language features in the text/s studied support my ideas?
- ☐ refer to specific textual evidence to support my ideas?
- ☐ develop ideas logically and use appropriate structure and language?

What are two strengths of my response?

____

____

What area/s of my response do I need to refine further?

____

____

____

____

UNIT
03

Widening the lens on the past, present and future

Inquiry question:
How can texts widen our perspective on the past, present and future of Aboriginal and Torres Strait Islander peoples?

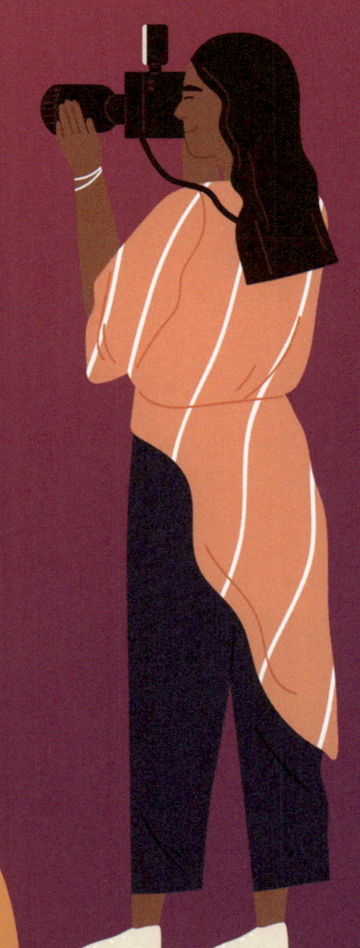

In this unit, students will explore how texts reflect alternate perspectives on Australia's history since European colonisation. They will consider how **representations** of colonisation are impacted by **perspective** and **context**, as well as how **symbolism** is used in contemporary texts to present varied perspectives on Australia's past. Students will explore how texts reflect Australia's present challenges of racial tension and discrimination. They will look at futuristic texts that invite audiences to challenge past and present perspectives in order to move towards a more unified country. Students will demonstrate their understanding through representation and analytical responses.

To address the focus inquiry question of the unit, students will engage with learning in three chapters:

CHAPTER 7

Rethinking the past

In this chapter, students will explore how representations of past colonisation are influenced by perspective and context by examining texts across a variety of modes. To do this, students will be guided through an analysis of *The Rabbits* by John Marsden and Shaun Tan, and respond by representing their own perspective on Australia's history.

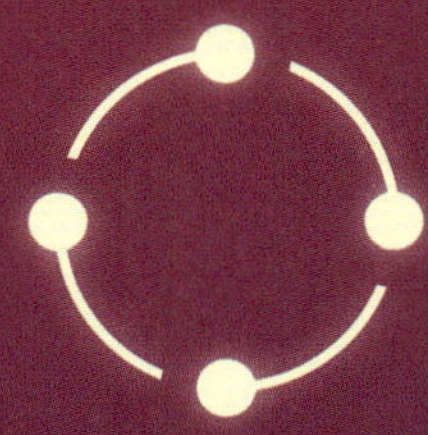

CHAPTER 8

Challenging our present

In this chapter, students will explore how perspectives on Aboriginal and Torres Strait Islander peoples are changing yet are also influenced by past events and representations. They will consider how texts represent experiences of racial tension and discrimination that emerge from prejudices, stereotypes and assumptions, and how texts reflect the challenges and impacts of this discrimination.

CHAPTER 9

Looking after our future

In this final chapter, students will examine futuristic texts that invite audiences to reconsider Australia's future. They will consider what we can learn from these texts about our connection to land and also why empathy is necessary in building a more unified future for Australia.

The learning activities within each chapter and the summative assessment options (on pages 120-121) provide opportunities to assess student achievement of the following outcomes and content points.

Outcome and focus area	Content point
EN4-RVL-01	**Reading, viewing and listening for meaning**
Reading, viewing and listening to texts	Engage with the ways texts contain layers of meaning, or multiple meanings Identify and understand that relevant prior knowledge and personal experience enables and enhances understanding when reading, viewing or listening to texts Explain how the use of language forms and features in texts might create multiple meanings Using a range of texts, describe how Aboriginal and Torres Strait Islander authors convey connections between Culture and identity
	Reflecting
	Discuss and reflect on the value of reading for personal growth and cultural awareness Reflect on how reading promotes a broad and balanced understanding of the world and enables students to explore universal issues Reflect on own experiences of reading by sharing what was enjoyed, and discussing challenges to strengthen an understanding of the value of reading
EN4-URA-01	**Representation**
Understanding and responding to texts A	Explore how language and text are acts of representation that range from objective to subjective and may offer layers of literal or implied meanings, and apply this understanding in own texts
	Connotation, imagery and symbolism
	Apply knowledge of how different patterns and combinations of figurative language devices can shape meaning throughout a text through established or dynamic associations, and experiment with these devices in own texts Explain how Aboriginal and Torres Strait Islander authors use figurative language and devices to shape meaning

EN4-URB-01 **Understanding and responding to texts B**	**Perspective and context** Explore how the perspectives of audiences shape engagement with, and response to, texts Consider the influence of cultural context on language Explore how specific elements of languages and dialects, including Standard Australian English, Auslan, Aboriginal and Torres Strait Islander Languages, and Aboriginal English, can shape expressions of cultural context in texts
EN4-ECA-01 **Expressing ideas and composing texts A**	**Representing** Compose visual and multimodal texts to represent ideas, experiences and values Select modal elements to work together to support meaning or shape reader response Use digital technologies where appropriate to compose multimodal texts
EN4-ECB-01 **Expressing ideas and composing texts B**	**Reflecting** Reflect on own composition of texts, using appropriate technical vocabulary to explain choices of language and structure in line with the target audience and intended purpose Describe the pleasures, challenges and successes experienced in the processes of understanding and composing texts Consider how purposeful compositional choices are influenced by specific elements of model texts Reflect on own ability to plan, monitor and revise during the composition process, and how this shapes clarity and effect

CHAPTER 7: RETHINKING THE PAST

Chapter overview

In this chapter, you will explore how representations of past colonisation are influenced by perspective and context by examining texts across a variety of modes. You will also consider how symbolism can be used to widen our understanding of the impacts of European colonisation on Aboriginal and Torres Strait Islander peoples. To do this, you will be guided through an analysis of *The Rabbits* by John Marsden and Shaun Tan, and respond by representing your own perspective on Australia's history.

Success criteria: in this chapter, I will be successful when I can ...

- identify perspectives shown about Aboriginal and Torres Strait Islander peoples and their experience of colonisation in texts
- explain how perspective and context influence representations of European settlement
- analyse how symbolism is used to represent alternative perspectives
- represent my own perspective on Australia's history through symbolism.

Chapter inquiry questions

- How are representations of Australia's colonisation influenced by perspective and context?
- How can symbolism be used to widen our understanding of Australia's colonisation?

Key vocabulary

- colonisation
- representation
- perspective
- context
- symbolism
- allegory

How are representations of Australia's colonisation influenced by perspective and context?

Aboriginal and Torres Strait Islander peoples have inhabited Australia for at least 65,000 years. However, in 1788 the first European settlement was proclaimed in Sydney in what is known as the colonisation of Australia. The term **colonisation** refers to the process of taking control over the indigenous people of an area and forming a new settlement. In this unit, you will examine how this time in Australia's history has been represented and how these past representations impact our present and future.

3.7.1 Warm-up

Australia before European Settlement (pre-1788)

Think about what you already know about the European settlement of Australia. Discuss what you know with a small group.

Now engage in some research about what Australia was like before settlement. Consider this from two points of view: the European settlers and Aboriginal and Torres Strait Islander peoples. Complete the table below with your notes.

How European settlers viewed life in Australia	How Aboriginal and Torres Strait Islander peoples viewed life in Australia

In his book *Talking to My Country*, Stan Grant shares his personal perspective on his experience growing up as a Wiradjuri and Kamilaroi man and the way history was taught to him. Read his words.

Talking To My Country

by Stan Grant

I was born into [a time] … called the 'great Australian silence'. It was the period of forgetting. The myths we created fed Australia's lie: that no blood had stained the wattle … [the land] was empty; tamed and claimed. These were the myths of my childhood, the myths of my education.

DISCUSS

Reflect on Grant's words. Do you think we still live in the 'great Australian silence'? What do we know now about the history of Australia long before European settlement?

There have been many **representations** of Australia's colonisation, and in this section of the chapter you will examine how some of these representations are influenced by **perspective** and **context**. First, let's define some important words.

Representation	Perspective	Context
Representation is the depiction of a thing, person or idea in a text. Depictions are deliberate and influenced by the values, beliefs and views of the creator.	A perspective is a lens through which we see the world – that is, the view of the subject that the creator of a text wants us to see. Perspective is created through the language choices in a text.	Context is the collection of factors that influence the creation of a text and the way it is received by audiences. Creators may be influenced by social, historical, political or personal values or attitudes. Responders may 'fill in the blanks' with what they already know from context as well as their values and beliefs.

Representations of Australia's colonisation are heavily influenced by perspective and context. We will now examine some texts that demonstrate this relationship.

DISCUSS

Go back to your response to the Warm-up activity. Talk with a partner about how context influenced the European settlers' perspective on Australia before colonisation in comparison with the reality for Aboriginal and Torres Strait Islander peoples.

Here are two representations of European settlement in the form of artworks. Examine them closely and consider how they have been influenced by perspective and context.

Landing of Captain Cook at Botany Bay, 1770	***We Call Them Pirates Out Here***
E. Phillips Fox (1902)	**Daniel Boyd (2006)**

3.7.2 Understanding and responding to texts B 

1 Research the context of each artist. Also research the time period of the creation of each artwork.

2 Complete the table below to identify the representation, perspective and context of each artwork.

	Landing of Captain Cook at Botany Bay, 1770	*We Call Them Pirates Out Here*
Representation How are European settlers and First Nations people represented in the artwork?		
Perspective What is the perspective on European settlement shown in the artwork?		
Context What contextual factors have influenced this artwork?		

3 **What is your perspective on European settlement? What contextual factors do you think have influenced your perspective?**

____

____

____

The representation of the impacts of Australia's colonisation on Aboriginal and Torres Strait Islander peoples is also heavily influenced by perspective and context. It is important that we see varied and sometimes confronting representations of these impacts to truly understand the ongoing effects for Aboriginal and Torres Strait Islander peoples.

Read the extract from *Sister Heart* by Sally Morgan, a verse novel written about a young Aboriginal girl who is taken from her family and sent to live in a government-run institution.

DISCUSS

What do you know about the Stolen Generation? Discuss this with your peers and research this topic to widen your understanding.

Sister Heart

by Sally Morgan

I'm taken
to a government place
given
to a government man
sitting
in a government chair
hard eyes staring.

Hmm, you're a thin little thing
Well now
let me see
what Reverend Dale has written.

He gazes at the paper
Ah yes
the Reverend has given you
the name of Anne
He glances up
What about Annie, instead?

INTERPRET

Discuss with a partner the structure of the lines in this stanza. What does this tell you about the character?

INTERPRET

Discuss with a partner why some sections are italicised in this extract. Describe the tone of these sections.

He waits
Not talking, Annie?

He glances at the paper
You spoke English on the station
It won't be long
before you are talking
to the other children
Go along with Nurse
make some new friends
this is your home now

My hands squeeze into fists

This
is
not
my
home

INTERPRET

Discuss with a partner the structure of the lines in this stanza. What perspective does this reflect?

3.7.3 Reading, viewing and listening to texts

Reflect on your reading. How has this extract from *Sister Heart* widened your perspective on the impacts of colonisation on Aboriginal and Torres Strait Islander peoples?

______

______

______

______

______

______

How can symbolism be used to widen our understanding of Australia's colonisation?

One way in which texts can widen our understanding of Australia's colonisation and its impacts is through **symbolism**. Symbols can be used by the creator of a text to convey perspectives. Audiences draw on their contextual understanding and experience of a symbol to draw a deeper meaning from the text.

> **VOCABULARY**
>
> **symbolism**
> *noun:* occurs when an object, character or place is used to show a larger idea, action or feeling. Usually, a reader draws on what they already know about a symbol to make the connection to a larger idea. For example, a bird flying could be a symbol of freedom.

To illustrate this idea, we will closely examine sections of the picture book *The Rabbits* by John Marsden and Shaun Tan.

DISCUSS

Research the artistic style of Shaun Tan. What makes his work so distinctive (unique)?

On the surface, the story is told from the perspective of marsupial creatures that see the arrival of a colony of rabbits. At first the rabbits are friendly, but soon they invade the country, destroy the environment, build their own houses, make the marsupials sick and take their children away. The marsupials try to fight back but are overpowered by the number of rabbits and their access to better technology. The picture book is considered an **allegory** that conveys deep concerns about the impact of colonisation on society and the environment.

> **VOCABULARY**
>
> **allegory**
> *noun:* a story that conveys a more symbolic meaning or moral message than its literal events.

3.7.4 Reading, viewing and listening to texts

1 Research the storyline of the picture book in more detail. If you can, read the picture book in its entirety.

2 From what you have read of the story, in what ways is it similar to Australia's colonisation and its impacts on Aboriginal and Torres Strait Islander peoples?

____

____

____

3 Why do you think rabbits have been chosen to symbolise the invading colony?

Look closely at this extract from the picture book, which shows the arrival of the rabbits. Then complete the activity that follows to demonstrate your understanding of the perspective offered in this image.

3.7.5 Understanding and responding to texts A

1 Describe what you can see in the extract above.

2 Explain how size is used to symbolise a perspective about colonisation.

3 Compare this image with the artworks you examined earlier in this chapter (*Landing of Captain Cook at Botany Bay, 1770* and *We Call Them Pirates Out Here*). As you consider this comparison, what perspective on colonisation do you think Marsden and Tan suggest in *The Rabbits*?

Examine the following extract from the picture book, which represents the impact of the rabbits' colonisation on the environment.

3.7.6 Understanding and responding to texts A

1 What perspective does this extract offer about the impact of colonisation on the environment?

2 Explain how the image uses colour symbolism to convey this perspective.

3 The text on this page reads 'The land is bare and brown and the wind blows empty across the plains'. The famous poem *My Country* by Dorothea Mackellar (1908) refers to Australia as a 'land of sweeping plains'. Find and read a copy of this poem online and discuss the differences between her representation of Australia and the one in this extract from *The Rabbits*. Why are they so different?

One of the most significant benefits of engaging with a range of texts that present varied representations of Australia's colonisation is that your own perspective can widen and develop further. Think about how your perspective on Australia's colonisation has been challenged or has widened to consider this experience more deeply.

3.7.7 Expressing ideas and composing texts A & B

1 Create a multimedia presentation to reflect one aspect of Australia's colonisation. In your representation, include:

- a collection of images that symbolically reflect a perspective about colonisation
- music to create a mood that reflects your chosen perspective
- minimal text – the focus should be on images and music.

2 In your presentation, briefly explain how two of your chosen images and the music used in your multimedia presentation represent a perspective about Australia's colonisation.

3.7.8 Chapter reflection

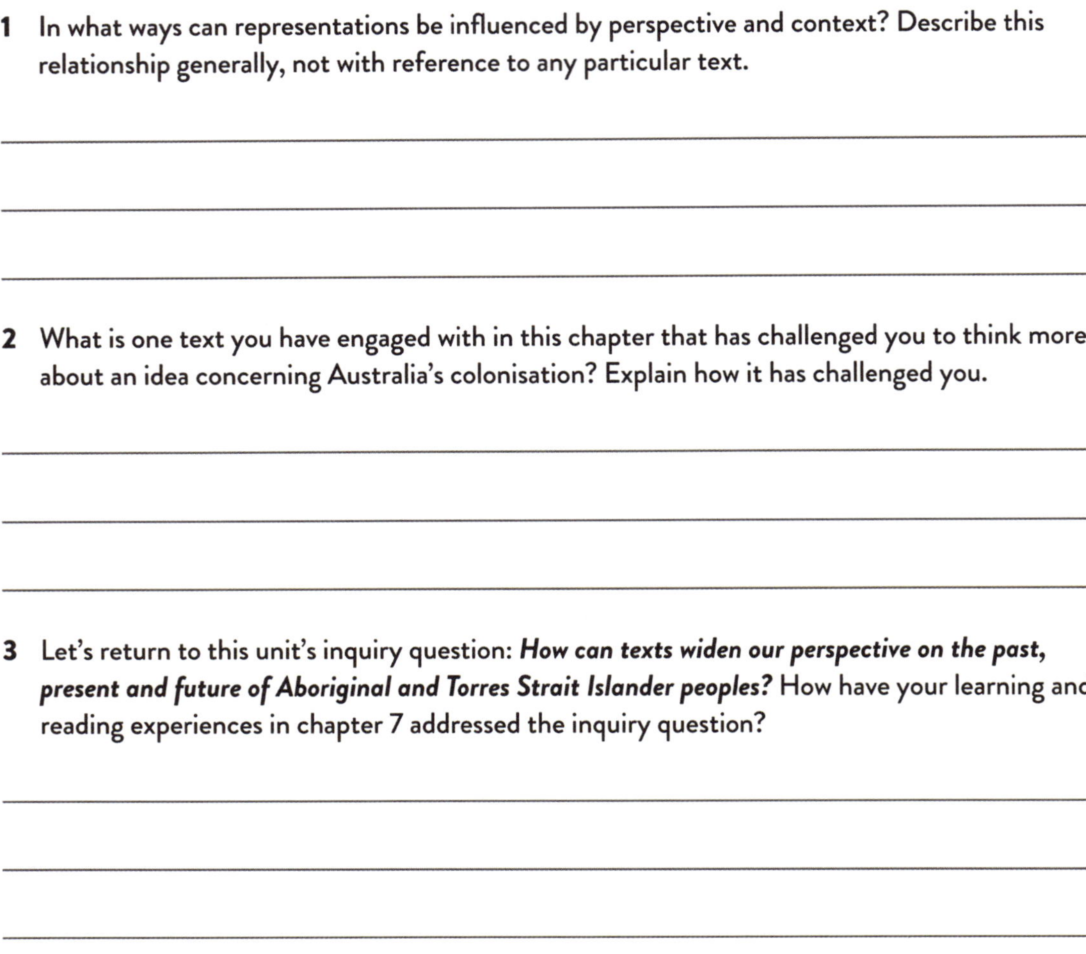

1 In what ways can representations be influenced by perspective and context? Describe this relationship generally, not with reference to any particular text.

2 What is one text you have engaged with in this chapter that has challenged you to think more about an idea concerning Australia's colonisation? Explain how it has challenged you.

3 Let's return to this unit's inquiry question: ***How can texts widen our perspective on the past, present and future of Aboriginal and Torres Strait Islander peoples?*** How have your learning and reading experiences in chapter 7 addressed the inquiry question?

CHAPTER 8: CHALLENGING OUR PRESENT

Chapter overview

In this chapter, you will explore how perspectives on Aboriginal and Torres Strait Islander peoples are changing, yet also influenced by past events and representations. You will consider how texts reflect experiences of racial tension and discrimination that emerge from prejudices, stereotypes and assumptions, and the impact of this discrimination. You will examine a range of texts that both represent these experiences and challenge society to move towards reconciliation.

Success criteria: in this chapter, I will be successful when I can ...

- identify how perspectives on Aboriginal and Torres Strait Islander peoples are changing from past representations
- explain how present perspectives are influenced by past contexts and representations
- analyse how texts reflect the experience of ongoing racial tensions and discrimination in our present context
- represent my own perspective on Australia's current landscape.

Chapter inquiry questions

- How are perspectives on Aboriginal and Torres Strait Islander peoples changing?
- How can we challenge the influence of past representations of Aboriginal and Torres Strait Islander peoples in our present context?
- What is the impact of ongoing racial discrimination?

Key vocabulary

- reconciliation
- stereotypes and assumptions
- prejudice
- racial tension
- discrimination

How are perspectives on Aboriginal and Torres Strait Islander peoples changing?

In 1995, the National Inquiry into the Separation of Aboriginal and Torres Strait Islander Children from Their Families was established. Following this inquiry, the *Bringing Them* Home report was released in 1997. This report outlined the grief and loss that was experienced by Aboriginal and Torres Strait Islander peoples, caused by past actions and events following colonisation.

3.8.1 Warm-up

Australia's present context

1 Research some facts and statistics about the population in our present context of Aboriginal and Torres Strait Islander peoples. Research areas such as percentage of Australia's population, access to education, healthcare, rates of illness, life expectancy and other areas that you come across in your research.

2 Discuss your findings in a small group.

3 Complete the 'Connect, Extend, Challenge' thinking routine in the table.

Connect How is your research connected to what you already know?	Extend What new ideas did you get that widened your thinking?	Challenge What challenges or problems have emerged for you?

The *Bringing Them Home* report (1997) found that:

> For individuals, their removal as children and the abuse they experienced at the hands of the authorities, or their delegates, have permanently scarred their lives. The harm continues in later generations, affecting their children and grandchildren.

Use the QR code to access the Bringing Them Home *interactive website hosted by the Australian Human Rights Commission. Explore the website and some of its links. Complete the following activity to reflect on your viewing experience.*

3.8.2 Reading, viewing and listening to texts

1 What perspective does the website reflect about the present context of Aboriginal and Torres Strait Islander peoples?

____

____

____

2 How does the website promote an interactive and engaging experience for users?

____

____

____

____

A key recommendation of the *Bringing Them Home* report was that a national apology be issued to Aboriginal and Torres Strait Islander peoples. In 2008, Kevin Rudd, then Prime Minister of Australia, issued this apology in Parliament. This National Apology is considered a landmark step towards **reconciliation** between Aboriginal and Torres Strait Islander peoples and non-Indigenous Australians.

VOCABULARY

reconciliation
noun: strengthening the relationship between Aboriginal and Torres Strait Islander peoples and non-Indigenous Australians, while acknowledging past events and moving towards a more united future.

Read this extract from Kevin Rudd's National Apology speech. You may also like to find this speech online and listen to Rudd's delivery of the speech in its entirety.

National Apology

by Prime Minister Kevin Rudd

Today we honour the Indigenous peoples of this land, the oldest continuing cultures in human history.

We reflect on their past mistreatment.

We reflect in particular on the mistreatment of those who were Stolen Generations – this blemished chapter in our national history.

The time has now come for the nation to turn a new page in Australia's history by righting the wrongs of the past and so moving forward with confidence to the future.

We apologise for the laws and policies of successive Parliaments and governments that have inflicted profound grief, suffering and loss on these our fellow Australians.

We apologise especially for the removal of Aboriginal and Torres Strait Islander children from their families, their communities and their country.

For the pain, suffering and hurt of these Stolen Generations, their descendants and for their families left behind, we say sorry.

To the mothers and the fathers, the brothers and the sisters, for the breaking up of families and communities, we say sorry.

And for the indignity and degradation thus inflicted on a proud people and a proud culture, we say sorry.

LANGUAGE

Label examples of metaphor. What impact do these metaphors have on audiences?

LANGUAGE

Circle examples of inclusive language. What does this type of language suggest about what is needed for reconciliation?

LANGUAGE

Underline examples of repetition. Why is this repetition so powerful?

3.8.3 Understanding and responding to texts B

1 Describe the tone of Rudd's apology speech. Refer to textual evidence and at least one language feature to support your description.

2 How is Rudd's choice of language in this speech influenced by his context?

3 The speech was delivered in 2008. Research what other events or initiatives have occurred since this time to progress towards reconciliation.

How can we challenge the influence of past representations of Aboriginal and Torres Strait Islander peoples in our present context?

Although steps towards reconciliation have been initiated at a national level, texts show us that past representations of Aboriginal and Torres Strait Islander peoples continue to influence our present context. It is important that all Australians continue to read, view and listen to the words of Aboriginal and Torres Strait Islander peoples themselves, as we seek to challenge these past representations and better understand the Australia of the present.

Some texts created by Aboriginal and Torres Strait Islander people explore how past events and long-held **stereotypes** and **assumptions** have continued to fuel **racial tensions** and **discrimination** in Australia's present. A stereotype is a widely held or generalised idea about a person or a group of people. Similarly, an assumption is a belief that a person has about an idea that has not been tested or proven. Many of the **prejudices** that exist today about Aboriginal and Torres Strait Islander peoples are influenced by past representations and horrific experiences of discrimination.

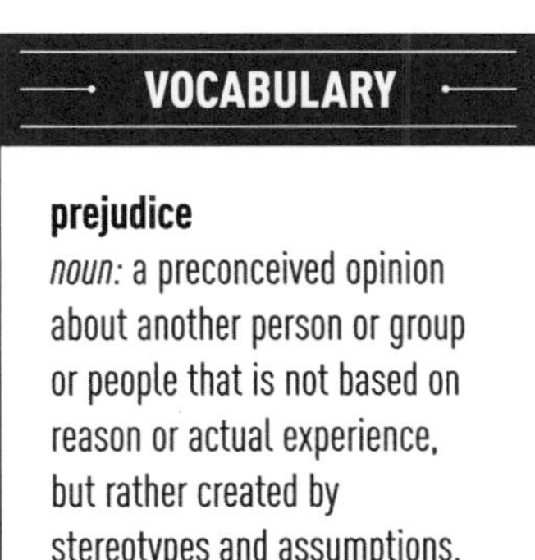

VOCABULARY

prejudice
noun: a preconceived opinion about another person or group or people that is not based on reason or actual experience, but rather created by stereotypes and assumptions.

Jack Davis' play *Honey Spot* exposes negative intergenerational assumptions about Aboriginal and Torres Strait Islander peoples – that is, assumptions about Aboriginal and Torres Strait Islander peoples that have been passed down from generation to generation over time. In the play, Tim, a young Aboriginal boy, and Peggy, a young non-Indigenous girl, meet in the forest and become friends. Peggy asks Tim to help her with a dance for an audition. Meanwhile, Peggy's father, the forest ranger, fears for her safety because of her involvement with Tim's family. He displays prejudice against Tim's brother William, whom he wants to punish for cutting down trees to make a didgeridoo. Peggy is caught between the prejudices of her father and her friendly experiences with Tim and his family.

Read an extract from the opening scene of the play. Tim is holding a piece of honeycomb when Peggy comes across him the forest. Look closely at how the characters respond to each other during their first meeting.

Honey Spot

by Jack Davis

PEGGY: Hello?
TIM: Go away!
PEGGY: What for?
TIM: Go away!
PEGGY: Are you all right?
TIM: Yeah.
PEGGY: What's wrong with you?
TIM: Nothing. Mind your own business.
PEGGY: Are you hiding from someone?

[Tim springs to his feet, threatening her with his tomahawk.]

TIM: Clear out, will ya.

[Peggy sees that he has honey all over the front of his shirt.]

PEGGY: Yuk! You've been lying in something.
TIM: Stop being a sticky beak, will ya?
PEGGY: It's honey.
TIM: No, it's not.
PEGGY: I know what you've been doing.

3.8.4 Understanding and responding to texts A

Consider the representations of Tim and Peggy in this opening extract. Complete the table to document your response to their character representation.

	See What do you see about their behaviour? Give textual evidence.	**Lens** Consider this experience through the lens of this character. Why do they act this way?	**Reflect** What do you think Davis wants to suggest through this representation?
Tim			
Peggy			

Despite their hostile introduction, Peggy and Tim become friends after they start talking to each other and she warns him that her dad, the Ranger, has said he will throw Tim's family out of their Forestry-owned cottage if he catches them chopping down trees in the forest. Peggy sees Tim dancing and she is inspired by Aboriginal music.

In the next extract, Peggy challenges her dad after hearing some of his prejudices. Read this extract and consider the Ranger's response to Peggy's questioning.

PEGGY: Daddy ...
RANGER: Yes?
PEGGY: Are you a racist?
RANGER: Am I a what?
PEGGY: Are you a racist?
RANGER: Good Lord, whatever made you think of a thing like that?
PEGGY: Well you don't seem to like some people.
RANGER: Go on.
PEGGY: You don't seem to like Aborigines.
RANGER: Some of them are all right, I suppose. It's just some of them can't be trusted.
PEGGY: Do you know any?
RANGER: Not personally. Now look, I know what you're getting at and it's got nothing to do with it. If anyone, black or white, is damaging the forest it's my job to ...
PEGGY: If you don't know any Aborigines how do you know they can't be trusted?
RANGER: Because everybody says so.

INTERPRET

Circle examples of prejudices, stereotypes and assumptions in the text.

INTERPRET

Underline a section of the extract that shows that Peggy is challenging her dad's racist views. Discuss with a partner the tone of Peggy's dialogue in the section you've chosen.

INTERPRET

Discuss with a partner one section of this conversation that has emotionally impacted you.

PEGGY: White people say so?

...

RANGER: Now look, Peggy, you really shouldn't get too friendly with these people.

PEGGY: Why not?

RANGER: Well, it's not their fault ... we've done some bad things to them in the past ...

PEGGY: Yes?

RANGER: Well, some things just don't mix. They're not like us. They have different habits, they live differently ... and I'm sure they wouldn't feel comfortable coming to this house.

PEGGY: How do you know? You don't know any Aborigines.

...

RANGER: But Peggy, they might do something to you, steal things, anything ...

PEGGY: Oh Daddy, I'm so glad you're not a racist!

3.8.5 Expressing ideas and composing texts A and B

1 With a partner, create and perform a tableau that reflects the extract you have read between Peggy and her father. A tableau is a representation of a dramatic scene, posing silently and without moving. Consider how you might use your body to represent the two characters in this scene and their views towards Aboriginal and Torres Strait Islander peoples.

2 After viewing a range of tableaux from other groups, reflect on how important this conversation is between Peggy and her father in challenging the influence of prejudices on the present context of Aboriginal and Torres Strait Islander peoples.

Despite her father's views, Peggy continues to see Tim and his family. She asks him to help her with her audition dance and Tim's mother helps them create a dance combining traditional ballet and corroboree dance styles. Look at this extract near the end of the text when they finally learn to embrace each other's dance styles and form a new style together.

MOTHER: All right, let's try again. Maybe we gotta have another think. We got two different styles of dancing, right? So if we want to do something together we both gotta bend a bit, so's the two dances can blend together.
PEGGY: Well what if we tried modern dance, like this ...

[She demonstrates a modern dance movement which incorporates elements of Aboriginal dance. Tim and William join in enthusiastically ...]

3.8.6 Understanding and responding to texts A

1 Mother says, 'If we want to do something together we both gotta bend a bit.' What do you think this means more broadly for Australian society?

____

____

____

2 How does Davis use dance to symbolise the way forward for both cultures? Refer to textual evidence to support your response.

____

____

____

____

What is the impact of ongoing racial discrimination?

While texts can show the importance of challenging prejudices as an important step towards reconciliation, they can also reflect the impacts of ongoing racial discrimination to widen the lens on the experience of Aboriginal and Torres Strait Islander peoples in our current context.

Read this opening extract from *The Boy from the Mish* by Gary Lonesborough. In the extract, Jackson and his friends are in a car driving away from the pub when they are approached by police.

The Boy from the Mish

by Gary Lonesborough

In the side-view mirror I see the police car slow, then pull over to the side of the road. They spin around and now they're coming, speeding up behind us. It's Constable Rogers. I'd recognise those big ears of his anywhere.

'No sudden movements, lads,' Kalyn jokes as he watches the rear-view mirror. Jarny ashes his cigarette on the interior armrest of the door. The cops' lights come on and spray red and blue into the car. Kalyn flicks on his blinker with a sigh and pulls over. My heart is pounding.

The doors of the police car open as Kalyn turns off the engine. Constable Rogers comes to Kalyn's window with his breathalyser in hand. He peeks inside, with his clean blue uniform over his body and his hat on his head.

'Kalyn, Jackson and Jarny,' he says, with such dissatisfaction. 'What are you boys doing? Mouthing off at the fellas in the pub?'

'Nah,' Kalyn says, 'just saying hello.'

'Is that right?' Constable Rogers says, his voice dropping an octave. 'Seemed a bit to me like youse were trying to start trouble.'

'Nope. No trouble,' Kalyn replies.

The other copper approaches my side of the ute, red-faced, walking slow, eyes searching through the open windows until he stops by me, staring me down. Constable Rogers holds up his breathalyser to Kalyn. Kalyn breathes into it before the breathalyser beeps.

'Looks like you're all good.'

I feel such a relief come over my body, even though I know Kalyn hasn't been drinking.

INTERPRET

Circle examples of prejudices, stereotypes and assumptions in the text.

INTERPRET

Examine the dialogue closely. What is the tone of the dialogue and what does this reflect about the characters?

INTERPRET

Discuss with a partner Jackson's response when they are cleared to go. What does this reflect about the impact of racial discrimination in today's society?

3.8.7 Reading, viewing and listening to texts

Reflect on how your reading of this extract from *The Boy from the Mish* may have challenged your views about the current context of Aboriginal and Torres Strait Islander peoples. Why do we need more representations like this in literature?

____

____

____

____

In 2013, prominent AFL player Adam Goodes was racially abused by a young teenager from the stands during a football game. This incident started a series of events that included Goodes being booed from the stands during matches in the last few years of his playing career. Headlines about the first and subsequent incidents appeared across the globe, forcing Australians to engage in difficult conversations about racial tensions in our current context.

DISCUSS

Research the Adam Goodes incident and the series of events that followed. Make sure you engage with several different sources. You should also pay close attention to the way language is used in various different ways to discuss this issue.

In 2019, two documentary films were made to represent Goodes' experience. The first is called *The Final Quarter* and focuses specifically on the last few years of Goodes' AFL career, beginning with the impact of the initial incident and examining its ongoing effect both on and off the field. The second film, called *The Australian Dream*, focuses on Goodes' life more broadly and his experiences of racial tension and cultural identity in Australia.

3.8.8 Understanding and responding to texts B

Find and view the film trailers for each of these documentary films online.

1 **What perspective do these films bring to the conversation about ongoing impacts of racial discrimination in Australia?**

2 **The trailer for *The Australian Dream* refers to 'casual racism'. Research this phrase and summarise its meaning.**

3 Have you witnessed, or experienced, an example of any form of casual racism? Describe this experience.

Extension activity

In 2014, Adam Goodes was named Australian of the Year. He delivered a historic speech calling for an end to racism to create a more united country. Find his speech online and analyse the way he uses language to evoke this perspective and call all members of the Australian population to share it.

3.8.9 Chapter reflection

What have you learned about the way past events have influenced the current context of Aboriginal and Torres Strait Islander peoples?

1 From your engagement with all texts in this unit, what overarching perspectives have you observed about the way forward towards reconciliation?

2 Let's return to this unit's inquiry question: ***How can texts widen our perspective on the past, present and future of Aboriginal and Torres Strait Islander peoples?*** How have your learning and reading experiences in chapter 8 addressed the inquiry question?

CHAPTER 9: LOOKING AFTER OUR FUTURE

Chapter overview

In this final chapter of the unit, you will examine how texts invite audiences to reconsider Australia's future. You will consider what we can learn from these texts about our connection to land and why empathy is necessary in building a more unified future for Australia. You will also compose texts to demonstrate your own perspective on Australia's future.

Success criteria: in this chapter, I will be successful when I can ...

- explain how texts written by Aboriginal and Torres Strait Islander writers represent their connection to country
- explain how perspectives on Australia's future are represented in texts
- analyse how texts invite audiences to reflect on Aboriginal and Torres Strait Islander peoples' future and the importance of empathy in building a more unified country
- represent my own speculations about Australia's future.

Chapter inquiry questions

- What does Australia's future for Aboriginal and Torres Strait Islander peoples look like?
- What can we learn from Aboriginal and Torres Strait Islander texts about our connection to land?
- Why is empathy important in building a unified Australian future?

Key vocabulary

- speculative fiction
- dystopian fiction
- empathy

What does Australia's future for Aboriginal and Torres Strait Islander peoples look like?

The previous chapters of this unit have examined representations of Aboriginal and Torres Strait Islander peoples since European colonisation and have considered ways in which these representations are changing. It is now time to look at what texts suggest about the future for Aboriginal and Torres Strait Islander peoples, and what is necessary in moving towards reconciliation and a more unified country.

3.9.1 Warm-up

Thinking about the future

Create a visual representation that demonstrates what you think the future for Aboriginal and Torres Strait Islander peoples looks like. Use one or more symbols to reflect the relationship between Aboriginal and Torres Strait Islander peoples and non-Indigenous Australians.

Read Stan Grant's words from his book Talking to My Country about the future of reconciliation in Australia.

Talking to My Country

by Stan Grant

For all that has divided us we are here together in a land that has become home to us all ... It should be easier from where they stand to grasp how profound our connection to country is. I would like to think that with a sense of place comes a sense of history; an acceptance that what has happened here has happened to us all and that to turn from it or hide from it diminishes us.

We seek solutions. We like to imagine that there is one elusive answer. Governments make policy and we bear the consequences. Of course there is no 'indigenous community' – we are many and our issues myriad and diverse. But we know that we also share our fate and our connection runs deep. There are those Australians of all colours and creeds who stand with us. They have marched over bridges, stood in silent protest, wept with apology. They are perhaps the majority – I hope they are. But there are bigots, those who would divide us, and if they are smaller in number their words land on us with the force of history.

LANGUAGE

Research the meaning of the following words from this extract: **profound**, **diminishes**, **elusive**, **myriad** and **bigots**.

LANGUAGE

Circle examples of inclusive language in the extract. What does this language imply for our future?

LANGUAGE

Underline examples of what Grant suggests is necessary for our future. Discuss these with a partner.

3.9.2 Reading, viewing and listening to texts

Reflect on your experience of reading this text. What do you think Grant sees as positive regarding the future of Aboriginal and Torres Strait Islander peoples? What changes do you think he would like to see happen?

____

____

____

____

____

____

In a report titled *Uluru Statement from the Heart*, Aboriginal and Torres Strait Islander peoples asked for more voice in policy matters concerning them. In October 2023, a national referendum asked the Australian population to vote on whether a Voice to Parliament for Aboriginal and Torres Strait Islander peoples would be permanently included in the Constitution. The Voice would have given advice to Parliament about matters relating to Aboriginal and Torres Strait Islander peoples. Read the words of Noel Pearson regarding the Voice.

On October 14, we whisper into the wind of time that 'No gets us nowhere and Yes makes it possible' ... On October 14, we can carve our generation's name into the bedrock of history ... And for as long as there is history in this land, it will be recorded – we were asked and we proudly voted Yes. We can do this for the love of our country. The love of Australia. My land. Your land. Our land.

DISCUSS

Engage in your own research about the Voice and the 2023 referendum. Explore the arguments made both for and against the change to the Constitution.

However, the majority of Australian people and Australian states voted 'No' in the referendum and the Voice was rejected. For some, this created uncertainty about the future of reconciliation in Australia. However, others believed that the referendum itself provided an opportunity for issues concerning Aboriginal and Torres Strait Islander peoples to be given more attention and conversation.

Use the QR code to access and read 'After the Voice referendum: how far along are First Nations treaty negotiations across the country?', an article published by The Conversation *in October 2023. Then complete the activity that follows.*

3.9.3 Understanding and responding to texts B

1 What perspective does the article offer about the future of Aboriginal and Torres Strait Islander peoples?

2 What contextual factors have influenced the representation of this perspective in the article?

3 Describe the tone of the article. What language choices contribute to this tone?

What can we learn from Aboriginal and Torres Strait Islander texts about our connection to land?

As we consider the future of Australia – not only regarding the relationship between Aboriginal and Torres Strait Islander peoples and non-Indigenous Australians, but also regarding the future of the land itself – we can continue to learn from Aboriginal and Torres Strait Islander writers about the importance of preserving connection to land.

Speculative fiction is a category of fiction that presents realities that are very different from our current world. The genre allows writers to imagine a world beyond our current context and present possibilities for our future. In doing so, writers can comment on issues in our world. A sub-genre of speculative fiction is **dystopian fiction,** in which the future is bleak and characterised by oppression and restriction. You may recognise popular dystopian texts such as *The Hunger Games* by Suzanne Collins, *Divergent* by Veronica Roth and the *Uglies* series by Scott Westerfeld.

The Interrogation of Ashala Wolf by Ambelin Kwaymullina is the first novel in a dystopian young adult fiction series called 'The Tribe'. The story is about a girl named Ashala. She is considered an 'Illegal', someone with extraordinary power. She is called a 'Sleepwalker', and like other Illegals, she is hunted by the government. She is tortured with a machine designed to reveal all her secrets, including the whereabouts of the rest of the Illegal Tribe.

DISCUSS

From your reading of the description of Kwaymullina's novel and your understanding of the importance of land and family to identity, what comment do you think the text is making on our future?

3.9.4 Understanding and responding to texts B

Examine each of the quotations from *The Interrogation of Ashala Wolf* in the table. Discuss how each quotation uses an Indigenous perspective to comment on the relationship between humans and the environment.

Quotation	How is an Indigenous perspective used to comment on the relationship between humans and the environment?
'I called out to the trees in my head. If I could make it back to you, I would.'	
'These trees grew from seeds that survived the great chaos. They carry within them the memories of their ancestors, the lost forests of the old world. They do not forget what humans have done.'	
'It [advanced technology] had isolated the people of the old world from nature, shielding them from the consequences of imbalance, and yet they'd believed, right up until the very end, that it would save them. But ... advances in technology could never compensate for failures in empathy.'	
'I stared up at the tuarts that towered over all the other plant life of the forest. They were so tall I could barely make out the tops, and so wide that Georgie and I would've had to join hands with about ten other people to circle the trunks.'	

Once Ashala is captured, the administrator, Neville Rose, and a scientist, Miriam Grey, use a machine to read Ashala's memories in the hope of finding the location of the Tribe. The machine propels her into a dreamlike world. Read the extract below, which describes what happens when Ashala is connected to the machine.

The Interrogation of Ashala Wolf

by Ambelin Kwaymullina

The world seemed to be receding around me as we entered the building that held the machine, or maybe it was me that was receding from the world, withdrawing into myself. I clung to that feeling of detachment, thankful for the sense of distance that made it seem like it was some other girl who was walking into a windowless room, drinking the vial of stay-awake liquid, and being strapped into the dreadful chair. Grey fussed over the box with Neville at her side, while Connor removed my collar, fitting the final restraint around my neck, and the hoop around my head. He retreated to stand beside the door, and I found myself bizarrely transfixed by his uniform, wondering why it had gone all fuzzy and sparkly around the edges. Then I realised that the entire room was filled with faintly blurring shapes and odd swirls of light.

... Neville approached to loom over the chair, distracting me from the starry ceiling. 'Is there anything you'd like to tell me before we begin, Ashala?'

'Yes,' I replied solemnly. 'Nothing ever truly ends, only transforms.'

3.9.5 Understanding and responding to texts A

1 How does reading this extract make you feel? Why do you feel this way? Refer to textual evidence to support your discussion.

2 What could the machine symbolise for Aboriginal and Torres Strait Islander cultures in Australia?

3 Discuss the significance of Ashala's final line for Aboriginal and Torres Strait Islander peoples: 'Nothing ever truly ends, only transforms.'

Why is empathy important in building a unified Australian future?

As outlined by Stan Grant in the extract earlier in this chapter, there is not one single solution to creating a more unified future for Aboriginal and Torres Strait Islander peoples and non-Indigenous Australians. There are many voices that make up the experience of being Australian, and like any group of people in society, Aboriginal and Torres Strait Islander peoples have diverse opinions and perspectives.

However, what is suggested through literature is the importance of **empathy** for the experience of Aboriginal and Torres Strait Islander peoples. Perhaps we can all build empathy by engaging in difficult conversations, sharing varied experiences, and opening up the dialogue about difference and diversity in our country. And perhaps from this empathy, we can move towards our future.

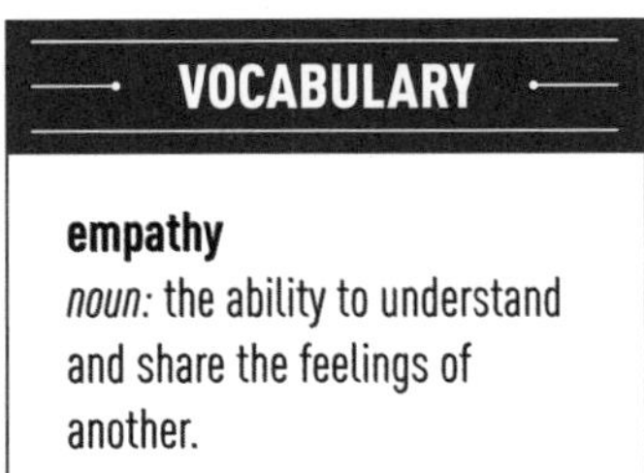

VOCABULARY

empathy
noun: the ability to understand and share the feelings of another.

Another speculative fiction novel, written by Noongarauthor Claire G. Coleman, is *Terra Nullius*.

DISCUSS

Research the term 'terra nullius'. In what context, related to Aboriginal and Torres Strait Islander peoples, has this term been used in Australia? In 1992, what decision did the High Court of Australia deliver about this term?

The opening half of the novel gives the impression that it is set in Australia in the early days of European settlement. Coleman does not state this, but as readers, we use our contextual knowledge of this part of history to make this assumption. We follow the story of Jacky, who is running away from a settler camp where he has experienced mistreatment at the hands of missionaries.

Coleman creates multiple perspectives in the novel. Read the extract below, which focuses on Sister Bagra's viewpoint as she learns that a letter of complaint has been written to the Church about the treatment of 'Native' children at the settlement.

Terra Nullius

by Claire G. Coleman

Who could have managed to send a letter to the Church back home, to the government, without her getting an inkling? ... Anyone who has trained animals would surely know that only a firm hand can teach them, that there is no use reasoning with animals. Even little children must be disciplined – a slap was so much more effective than any number of reasoning explanations. The Natives, never willingly growing away from their savagery, were animals. At most they were children. The only way to help them was to use training methods appropriate to what they were.

3.9.6 Reading, viewing and listening to texts

Reflect on your experience of reading this text. How does Coleman demonstrate the lack of empathy Sister Bagra has towards the children of the settlement?

Towards the middle of the novel, Coleman reveals a major twist. The 'Settlers' are in fact aliens who have come to Earth with advanced weapons and resistance to diseases. The 'Natives' are revealed to be the very few surviving humans left on Earth. The novels shifts into a science fiction world.

Read this next extract from *Terra Nullius*, in which Jacky comes across a settlement of Natives who are hiding from the Settlers, whom they call the 'Toads'. An old man at the settlement tells Jacky about the 'great society' that humans had once established before the Toads arrived. Consider how Coleman symbolically reflects the experience of her own people through this representation.

...the humans, had once created a great society, built great cities, farmed, engineered. Once his people, the humans, had controlled the entire planet as the Toads had for Jacky's entire memory. Looking at the world you could see the remains of the human presence: the old roads, the ruined buildings, traces of farms. Despite all that it was hard for him to believe that the humans he was seeing were capable of such things, of building worlds.

Humans had once enslaved other humans, decided their fate based on the colour of their skin. Racism, the old man had called it. When he described it Jacky was shocked. Humans were not nice people, humans had war and despair and theft even before the Toads arrived. The very land he walked on, the continent of Australia had been home to one of oldest cultures on the planet, maybe even the galaxy. Then a younger warlike culture had come and stolen their land, enslaved the people, killed thousands.

LANGUAGE

Label parts of the extract, particularly in the opening, that contradict the historical notion of 'terra nullius'.

INTERPRET

Underline any parts of the text in which you feel Coleman is drawing a parallel with the experience of Aboriginal and Torres Strait Islander peoples following Australia's colonisation.

The arrivals of the Toads had eliminated all racism and hate within the human species. It was not that with a common enemy the humans decided to work together – humans never made a decision to no longer fight between themselves. Instead the colonisation by the Settlers simply ended all discrimination within the human race by taking away all the imbalance. There was no caste or class within humans; to the Toads who now owned the planet and everyone on it all humans had the same low status. To the Toads, all humans were nothing more than animals.

3.9.7 Expressing ideas and composing texts A and B

1 **Write an analytical response that explains how Coleman uses symbolism in her speculative fiction text to provide a perspective about Australia.**

- Outline a perspective shown in the text in your topic sentence.
- Explain how symbolism is used to reflect this perspective.
- Refer to textual evidence from the extract to support your discussion.
- Develop your ideas logically.

2 **Return to the Warm-up activity earlier in this chapter. Following your reading of texts in this chapter, what could you add to, or enhance in, the visual representation you created about Australia's future?**

3.9.8 Chapter reflection

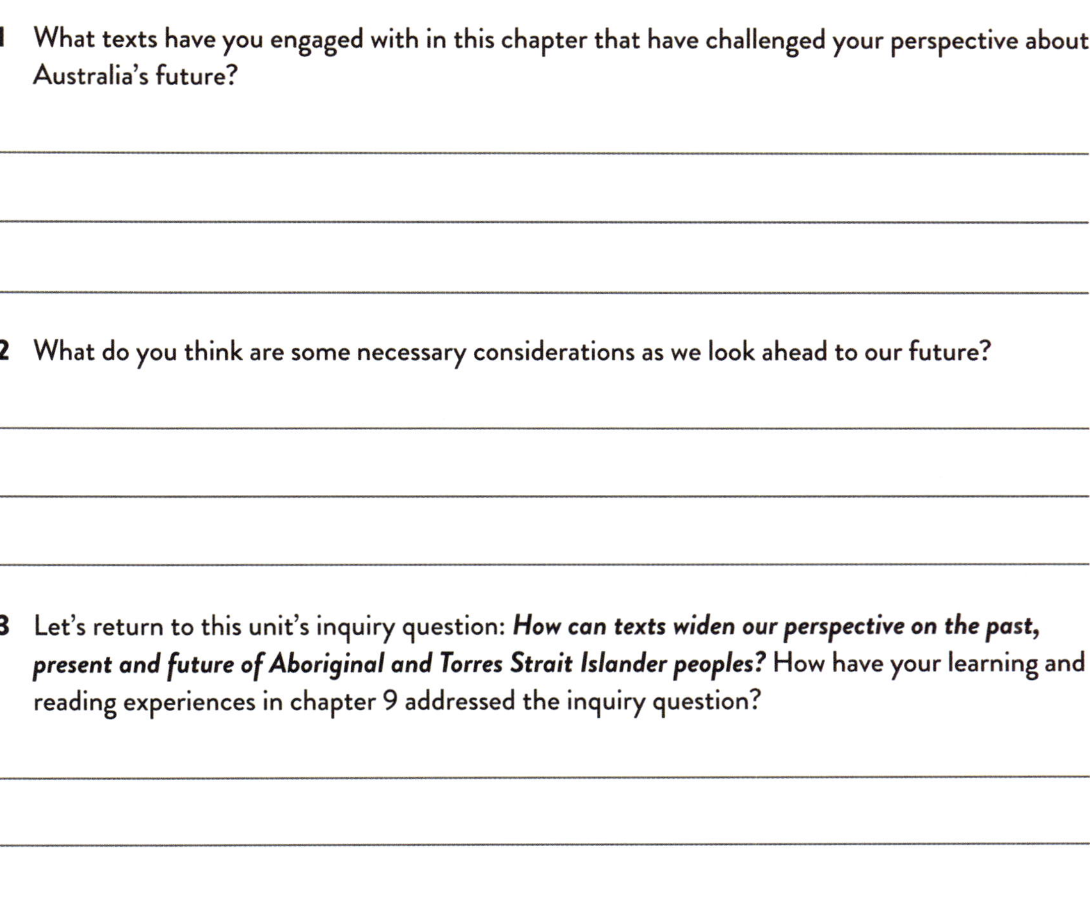

1 What texts have you engaged with in this chapter that have challenged your perspective about Australia's future?

2 What do you think are some necessary considerations as we look ahead to our future?

3 Let's return to this unit's inquiry question: ***How can texts widen our perspective on the past, present and future of Aboriginal and Torres Strait Islander peoples?*** How have your learning and reading experiences in chapter 9 addressed the inquiry question?

Unit 3: **Summative assessment**

The summative assessment options below provide opportunities to demonstrate your achievement of the following outcomes and content points.

Outcome and focus area	EN4-RVL-01 Reading, viewing and listening to texts	EN4-URA-01 Understanding and responding to texts A	EN4-URB-01 Understanding and responding to texts B	EN4-ECA-01 Expressing ideas and composing texts A	EN4-ECB-01 Expressing ideas and composing texts B
Content point	Reading, viewing and listening for meaning Reflecting	Representation Connotation, imagery and symbol	Perspective and context	Representing	Reflecting

Option 1:

Part A: Create a photo essay that demonstrates perspectives on Australia's past, present and future.

Ensure that your response:
- conveys clear **perspectives** about Aboriginal and Torres Strait Islander peoples relative to context
- uses **symbolic** images to convey these perspectives.

Part B: Compose a reflection that explains the choices you have made in your photo essay.

Ensure that your response:
- discusses how the **perspectives** presented are influenced by context
- explains how **symbolism** is used to shape the **representation** of **perspectives**
- **reflects** on how your **reading experiences** in this unit have shaped the formation of these perspectives.

Option 2:

Compose a reading and viewing reflection that discusses how engaging with three texts in this unit has shaped your understanding of the past, present and future for Aboriginal and Torres Strait Islander peoples.

For each text, select and include a symbolic image that reflects the perspective shown in the text.

Ensure that your response:
- discusses how the **perspective**s presented in the chosen texts are influenced by context
- uses **symbolic** images to convey these perspectives
- explains how **language** is used in each text to shape the **representation** of **perspectives**
- **reflects** on how your **reading experiences** in this unit have shaped the formation of these perspectives.

Option 3:

Create and present a TED Talk-style presentation that discusses how your knowledge of Aboriginal and Torres Strait Islander peoples has been enhanced or changed through your reading experiences.

In your presentation, select and include a range of symbolic images that demonstrate the perspectives you have gained. You must also refer to at least three texts that you have engaged with in this unit.

Ensure that your response:

- discusses how the **perspectives** presented in the chosen texts are influenced by context
- uses **symbolic** images to convey these perspectives
- explains how **language** is used in each text to shape the **representation** of **perspectives**
- **reflects** on how your **reading experiences** in this unit have shaped the formation of these perspectives.

Assessment as learning: self-assessment

Does my response:

- ☐ discuss the relationship between perspective and context?
- ☐ use symbolic images to reflect a variety of perspectives?
- ☐ analyse how language is used to shape the representation of perspectives?
- ☐ reflect on my personal experiences of reading, considering how my perspectives were challenged or enhanced?

What are two strengths of my response?

____

____

What area/s of my response do I need to refine further?

____

____

____

____

UNIT
04

Media, media, everywhere!

Inquiry question:
How do media texts have authority over their audience, and can they be trusted to present the truth?

In this unit, students will refine their **reading, viewing and listening** skills by applying a range of strategies to engage with media texts. They will explore how media texts create **authority** over their audience, including their ability to seize and maintain attention, evoke emotional responses and use interactive methods to promote engagement. Students will investigate the role media texts serve in our society to appreciate their **literary value**. Throughout the sequence of learning, students will develop their own **argument** about the ways in which media texts represent the truth. Students will express ideas through **speaking** and will also share informed ideas by writing **persuasive** compositions.

To address the focus inquiry question of the unit, students will engage with learning in three chapters:

CHAPTER 10

Seizing attention

In this chapter, students will explore how media texts such as newspapers, magazines and online news sites seize and maintain audience attention. They will examine how both written and visual language is used to attract audience attention and create a sense of authority over its audience.

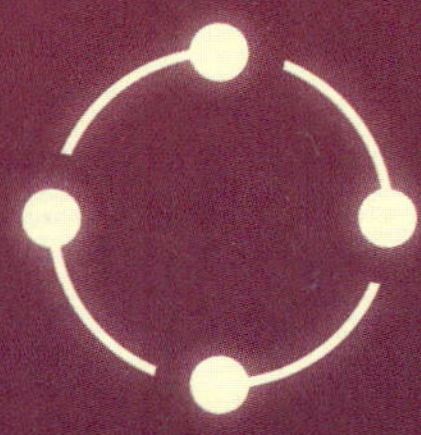

CHAPTER 11

Representing the truth

In this chapter, students will critically examine how media texts represent the truth. They will closely investigate the effect of bias in media texts and the way audience reception can be manipulated. Students will continue to examine how various written and visual language features are used to impact audience reception.

CHAPTER 12

Interactive engagement

In this final chapter, students will explore how media texts such as social media, podcasts and interactive websites promote more collaboration and agency for their audience. Students will develop arguments about the role of interactivity in media texts for modern audiences.

The learning activities within each chapter and the summative assessment options (on pages 160-161) provide opportunities to assess student achievement of the following outcomes and content points.

Outcome and focus area	Content point
EN4-RVL-01 **Reading, viewing and listening to texts**	**Reading, viewing and listening skills**
	Apply reading pathways to determine form, purpose and meaning Revisit texts to develop a clear understanding of the themes, ideas and attitudes they express
	Reading, viewing and listening for meaning
	Explore the main ideas and thematic concerns posed by a text for meaning Explain personal responses to characters, situations and issues in texts, recognising the role of written, oral or visual language in influencing these personal responses Understand how language use evolves over time and in different places and cultures, and is influenced by technological and social developments
EN4-URA-01 **Understanding and responding to texts A**	**Code and convention**
	Use appropriate metalanguage to describe how meaning is constructed through linguistic and stylistic elements in texts Understand how language forms, features and structures, in a variety of texts, vary according to context, purpose and audience, and demonstrate this understanding through written, spoken, visual and multimodal responses Analyse how texts can draw on the codes and conventions of a range of modes and media to shape new meanings, and demonstrate this understanding in own texts
EN4-URB-01 **Understanding and responding to texts B**	**Argument and authority**
	Understand how argument in text is constructed through specific language forms, features and structures, and apply this understanding in own texts Explain how the subjectivity or objectivity of arguments in texts is constructed through specific language forms, features and structures, and reflect on these in own texts Analyse how engaging personal voice is constructed in texts through linguistic and stylistic choices, and experiment with these choices in own texts Select and sequence appropriate evidence from texts and reliable sources to support arguments and build authority Understand how the authority of a text is constructed by the author's choices in content and style, and use this knowledge to influence the composition of own texts Examine how audiences can express degrees of authority over meaning in a text Understand that the authority of a text may be questioned through comparison with other texts

EN4-URC-01 **Understanding and responding to texts C**	**Literary value** Understand how texts from all modes and media can serve different personal, social and cultural purposes according to their form and context Describe how thematic and stylistic qualities of texts contribute to the ways they can be valued in different contexts
EN4-ECA-01 **Expressing ideas and composing texts A**	**Speaking** Use rhetorical strategies to engage an audience and evoke an emotional response Create a range of spoken, signed or communicated texts that express ideas and show an understanding of audience Participate in informal discussions about texts and ideas, including speculative and exploratory talk, to consolidate personal understanding and generate new ideas Use features of gesture, manner and voice to signal the progression and development of ideas through language and structure
	Text features: persuasive Compose persuasive texts that present arguments from a range of viewpoints, including their own, and that reflect a broadening understanding of perspectives beyond immediate experience Compose persuasive texts that include an opening or thesis to provide a definition and position, effectively sequenced elaboration paragraphs, and a conclusion that synthesises ideas, restates a position or makes a conclusion or recommendation Incorporate subjective and objective evidence to enhance and support elaboration of arguments Use rhetorical language to shape ideas and express a perspective or argument Provide counterargument and refutation where appropriate

CHAPTER 10: SEIZING ATTENTION

Chapter overview

In this chapter, you will explore how media texts such as newspapers, magazines and online news sites seize and maintain audience attention. You will examine how both written and visual language is used to attract audience attention and create a sense of authority over its audience.

Success criteria: in this chapter, I will be successful when I can ...

- describe the role media texts play in our world
- explain how media texts seize the attention of audiences
- analyse how the codes and conventions of media texts contribute to their authority
- use language persuasively to compose texts that attract audience attention.

Chapter inquiry questions

- What authority do media texts have in our world?
- How can a good headline attract audience attention and create authority over a text?

Key vocabulary

- media text
- authority over a text
- authority of a text
- headline
- codes and conventions

What authority do media texts have in our world?

There can be two ways to define a **media text**. The first meaning refers to the type of texts you have probably discussed before: texts that share or communicate messages or ideas that relate to a large group of people.

However, the second and more technical definition of a media text is specific to the term 'media', a plural form of the word 'medium'. This means the specific method of communication chosen to share ideas. Medium types might include newspaper, television, internet or radio.

Most media texts also use a combination of modes to communicate ideas. Some common modes are speaking, viewing, listening and reading. For example, the medium of television is a combination of viewing and listening modes.

4.10.1 Warm-up

My 24 hours of media

Complete the log below to identify examples of each type of media you have engaged with in the last 24 hours.

	Examples		Examples
Television		**Online media**	
Radio		**Social media**	
Print media		**Billboards**	

In this unit, you will investigate how media texts seize audience attention through a range of clever written and visual language choices. But first, let's clarify what a media text is and what its purpose is.

The purpose of a media text is usually to entertain, inform or persuade an audience. It is always important to closely examine the creator of the media text and think about what they will gain from sharing information with a specific audience. You will look at this more closely in chapter 11.

Media, media, everywhere!

Now that you know what is meant by 'media texts', let's examine the evolution of media texts. We know that humans have communicated messages and shared information since the dawn of time. Initially, this was mostly via oral storytelling. Some forms of written communication in prehistoric times included cave paintings and rock art. The Sumerian script, from around 3000 BCE, is considered the earliest known writing. In the fifteenth century, printing mediums were invented, which enabled mass methods of communication to be created such as books and other printed materials.

Extension activity

Research the origins and evolution of media texts, including important inventions and advancements in each century. Record your notes in this table.

Century	Important inventions and advancements	How did this change how information was communicated?
17th (1601–1700)		
18th (1701–1800)		
19th (1801–1900)		
20th (1901–2000)		
21st (2001–)		

There is no doubt that our world today is saturated with media texts. From the moment we wake up in the morning, we can be exposed to a range of different forms of media, all sharing different messages and information. Media texts infiltrate every aspect of life. From food advertisements that make us crave products to political campaigns that dictate the future of our country, media texts have **authority** in our world.

VOCABULARY

Authority
Authority, in the context of the English syllabus, has two meanings: **authority *over* a text** and **authority *of* a text**.

authority over a text refers to who controls the meaning in composing the text and receiving it. Usually, the creator of a text controls the meaning through the way they use language to present ideas and position the audience. However, media texts show us that sometimes a text has little meaning until audiences react to it and give it more meaning (e.g. an article 'goes viral' online and is shared by thousands of people).

authority of a text refers to how trustworthy the text is on the subject presented. The level of credibility may be assessed when comparing a media text with others to consider all perspectives.

DISCUSS

Discuss an example of a media text that you think demonstrates authority over a text. What is it about the way the text has been created that gives it this authority?

4.10.2 Reading, viewing and listening to texts

Find the trailer for the documentary film The Social Dilemma *online and watch it.*

1 What does the film suggest about how media texts have become a significant part of our society?

____

____

____

2 What does the film suggest about the role of both creators and the audience in establishing authority over media texts?

____

____

____

3 A film trailer is essentially an advertisement for the film itself, therefore this text is a form of persuasion. Do you think this film seems credible? How is authority of the text created in this film?

____

____

____

As you read previously, authority over a media text is dependent on both the creator of the text and the audience in the way they make meaning of the text. One way that we know media texts play a significant role in our world is the way language has evolved and how people are influenced by what they engage with.

4.10.3 Expressing ideas and composing texts A

You will now participate in an informal discussion with a group of your peers to speculate on the future of media texts. You will share your own ideas and build on the ideas of others in your group.

Your topic is: *What's next for media texts? What does the future of media look like?*

First, prepare some of your own ideas guided by the list below.

- Discuss what the evolution of media so far suggests about future advancements.
- Provide a theory of your own about how audiences will become more involved in making meaning in media texts.
- Question some current trends for media texts and challenge their role in the future.
- Draw on examples of media texts that support your ideas and opinions.

In your discussion, ensure that you consider how you use verbal and non-verbal language to show the progression and development of your ideas.

How can a good headline attract audience attention and create authority over a text?

In a world inundated with media texts, it is crucial to seize the attention of the audience and, more importantly, hold the audience's interest. The creators of media texts such as newspapers, online news articles, magazines, editorials and opinion pieces use **headlines** to capture a reader's attention. A headline is the heading at the top of an article that usually indicates the topic or content to be addressed in the article. Headlines are often short. They aim to attract readers so they feel inclined to read the entire article.. Look at the way these headlines have been devised to seize attention in different ways.

Kitten stuck up tree

Cat-astrophe!

Heroic firefighters risk lives for cat

Taxpayers foot the bill to save local cat

DISCUSS

Discuss the differences between these headlines. In what ways have they been devised to attract attention in different ways? What feelings does each headline evoke for readers?

VOCABULARY

codes and conventions
noun: the arrangement of language features and structures specific to a form of text that help create meaning. The codes and conventions help you recognise and create familiarity with the type of text you are reading. For example, the codes and conventions of a newspaper report are a headline, a lead paragraph, images, captions, quotes and descriptive and factual language.

Creators of media texts manipulate the **codes and conventions** of specific types of media to create these headlines, often aiming to evoke a certain response in the reader: intrigue, fear, excitement, curiosity, amusement, anger or passion, just to name a few. In doing so, authority over a text is created as meaning is controlled for the reader.

Let's look at some of the codes and conventions used to create attractive headlines for online news sites. For each feature, find and record an example from an online news article.

Feature	Example from an online news article
Rhetorical questions are asked without the intention of receiving an answer. They may be used by a headline to make a reader realise they are also questioning this same idea and need to engage with the article to learn more.	
Hyperbole is the use of exaggerated language. Headlines may exaggerate a scenario to make the reader feel more emotional about the topic, and maybe even shocked or challenged by an idea.	

Feature	Example from an online news article
A **play on words** occurs when a word or phrase with more than one meaning is used. A headline with a play on words may engage the reader through humour.	
Descriptive language is the use of a combination of adjectives and adverbs. Headlines may use this to force readers to visualise an experience or to position them to feel a certain way about a scenario.	

4.10.4 Understanding and responding to texts A

1 Examine each of the headlines listed in the table. Identify a code and convention used in the headline and explain how it seizes the attention of audiences.

Headline	Code and convention	How does it seize the attention of audiences?
Studies show that the study of Mathematics is something you can count on		
10 amazingly useful hacks for storing priceless photographs		
This balloon prank will change your life forever		
Is travelling business class worth the extra money?		

2 Choose one of the headlines above. What do you think the accompanying article might include to maintain the attention of the audience?

______

______

______

4.10.5 Expressing ideas and composing texts A

It is now your turn to create headlines that capture the attention of readers for each of the topics listed. Consider how you can use the codes and conventions explored in this chapter to persuade readers to give the article their attention.

Topic	Your headline
Cheating scandal at the Olympics	
Books to read in the summer holidays	
Town's exposure to toxic chemicals	
The discovery of a new species of frog	
Increasing rates of cyberbullying	

4.10.6 Chapter reflection

1 Outline your understanding of the authority of media texts in our world.

2 What role does language play in influencing the way people respond to media texts?

3 Let's return to this unit's inquiry question: ***How do media texts have authority over their audience, and can they be trusted to present the truth?*** How have your learning and reading experiences in chapter 10 addressed the inquiry question?

CHAPTER 11: REPRESENTING THE TRUTH

Chapter overview

In this chapter, you will critically examine how media texts represent the truth. You will closely investigate the effect of bias in media texts and the way audience reception can be manipulated. From this investigation, you will develop your own argument about the value of media texts in representing versions of the truth. You will continue to examine how various codes and conventions of media texts are used to impact audience reception and create authority. You will also compose persuasive responses that present your own arguments and perspectives.

Success criteria: in this chapter, I will be successful when I can …

- identify examples of bias in media texts
- explain how the codes and conventions of media texts can be manipulated to present alternate perspectives and representations
- critically analyse how a variety of media texts represent variations of the truth
- compose persuasive responses that reflect a personal argument about the value of media texts in sharing differing perspectives.

Chapter inquiry questions

- How is the authority of media texts impacted by bias?
- What value do media texts have in representing versions of the truth?

Key vocabulary

- purpose
- bias
- emotive language
- binary
- active and passive voice
- literary value
- argument

How is the authority of media texts impacted by bias?

You would have heard the expression that 'there are two sides to every story'. In our world of media texts, this expression could probably be updated to many more than just two sides. It is important that you engage with media texts with a critical eye, always considering the **purpose** of the text and what is influencing its composition. This will help you determine the credibility, or authority, of the text on the topic it presents. A text may be **biased** in favour of a certain perspective and may want you, the audience, to adopt a particular viewpoint.

VOCABULARY

bias
noun: heavy inclination towards a certain idea, either in favour or against it. A bias may be unfair or prejudicial, often not considering other points of view.

4.11.1 Warm-up

Same story, different versions

Choose a recent news story or a topic that has been discussed in the media lately. Find at least three different media texts that all present a similar idea about this topic. Record some observations in the table.

Topic/story:			
Media text title	Type of media	What aspect of the topic does this media text focus on?	What do you think the aim of this media text is?

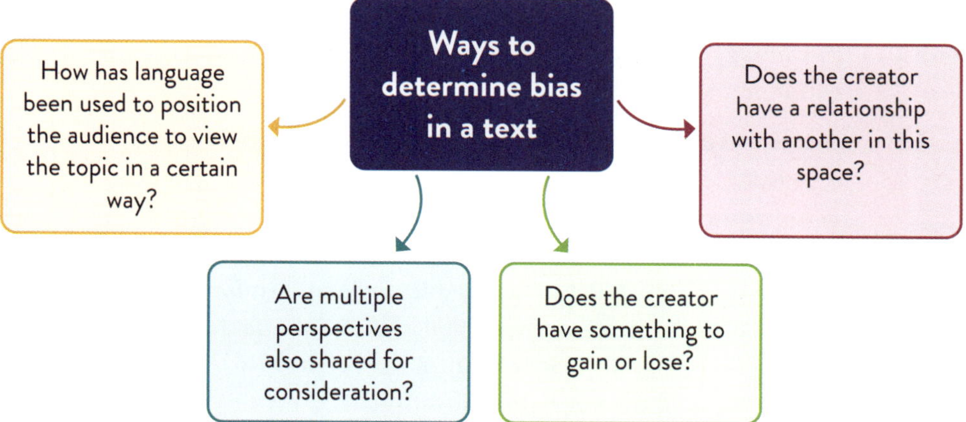

The diagram above outlines some questions that could be asked of a media text to determine bias. The line between fact and fiction in media texts can sometimes be blurred and very confused. Because of this, it could be said that there will always be some level of bias in any media text. Therefore, it is always important to critically examine the purpose of the text and know that you, as the audience of the text, must use your judgement to determine the 'truth'. Of course, truth can be regarded as subjective, as one person's 'truth' may not be true for another. So, in this context, determining the 'truth' refers to knowing how to discern the credibility or trustworthiness of ideas and opinions.

DISCUSS

Go back to the media texts you accessed in the Warm-up activity earlier in this chapter. Can you find any examples of bias in these texts?

A feature article is one type of media text that can present a very strong opinion on a single topic and try to persuade audiences to adopt a similar viewpoint. Often, these texts are biased towards certain ideas and use their codes and conventions to achieve this persuasion. **Emotive language**, **binaries** and **active and passive voice** are all used in feature articles to shape meaning and impact audience reception.

Emotive language	Binaries	Active and passive voice
The specific choice of words and phrases that have strong emotional associations in order to create the same emotional responses in the audience.	A binary is something that has two parts. In this context, media texts may create binaries by creating a divide between two opposing groups. Often one group is vilified (portrayed as 'the villain') while the other is glorified.	In active voice, the subject of the verb is doing the action, which may often place blame or responsibility on the subject. In passive voice, the subject of the verb is being acted on, which takes the attention away from the person involved.

Read the opening of the following feature article. Examine examples of these types of language and consider how they create bias in the article.

A binary is created between the 'chaos' of adults and the 'whispers' of children – suggesting that children are not listened to.

'catastrophe' evokes feelings of disaster and urgency.

'declared war' establishes a binary again between adults and children.

The heroes of the future: why ignoring children is endangering our planet

In a world drowning in the chaos of adult voices, there exists a whisper, a plea from the pure-hearted, innocent caretakers of our future – the children. Adults often ignore, dismiss and overlook the voices of youth, considering their insights about the future of the planet to be uneducated and ill-informed. However, as we stand at the precipice of climate catastrophe, it becomes undeniably clear that we've been deaf to the very voices that hold the key to our salvation.

In 2018, school students across Australia participated in a school strike to share their concerns about the future of our world. The sounds of the school yard spilled out into the streets, as students in their tens of thousands, inspired by the fearless activism of Greta Thunberg, declared war against national policymakers and their apathy towards climate strategies.

'Pure-hearted' and 'innocent' evoke a sense of guilt about the overlooked children.

Adults are positioned here as the villains who have ignored children. This binary is created using active voice, placing the blame on the adults.

This phrase is passively constructed to keep the focus on the students (who are written about in the active voice).

Extension activity

Write the opening of a feature article written by one of these 'national policymakers' that addresses the same issue: the voice of youth in matters concerning the environment. How might this article be written differently?

4.11.2 Understanding and responding to texts B

For this activity, you will read two feature articles written about the topic of gaming. The feature articles focus on different aspects of the topic.

The title of the first article is 'Curious Kids: Why do adults think video games are bad?' The title of the second article is 'Extremists use video games to recruit vulnerable youth. Here's what parents and gamers need to know'.

1 What do these titles suggest about the purpose of each article?

___

___

___

Use the QR codes to access and read the two feature articles.

2 Complete this table to summarise your observations of each article.

	'Curious Kids: Why do adults think video games are bad?'	'Extremists use video games to recruit vulnerable youth. Here's what parents and gamers need to know'
What is the main idea presented in the article?		
Who is the audience of the article and how does this influence the way it is written?		
Do you feel this article displays bias? If so, how is this bias created?		
What authority does this article have on this topic? Provide evidence to support your answer.		

3 Which article do you feel has more authority on this topic? Explain your answer.

4.11.3 Expressing ideas and composing texts A

It is now your turn to write the opening of a feature article – but with a twist!

Examine the writing scenario below and read the descriptions of the two media outlets underneath it.

You and a partner are to write the openings of two different feature articles. One is to be published by Media outlet 1, and one by Media outlet 2. You must write a headline and two opening paragraphs that display bias according to the perspective you are writing from.

- Write a headline and two opening paragraphs that display bias and persuade your readers.
- Use emotive language, binaries and active and passive voice, plus other language features, to create this bias.
- Logically sequence the introduction of your ideas.

The scenario: a high-rise apartment building is being planned for an already over-populated suburb. Residents are concerned that there is not enough infrastructure to support more people in the area, such as facilities, transport, schools and access to healthcare. The location of the proposed building would also mean the loss of local flora and fauna.	
Media outlet 1 has a share in the building company that has won the contract to build the proposed apartment building, if approved.	Media outlet 2 has strong links with a local wildlife organisation and has sponsored their fundraising events for a number of years.

Write your version of the feature article headline and opening here. Write at least two short paragraphs of the article here or in your English notebook.

What value do media texts have in representing versions of the truth?

In this part of the chapter, you will begin to develop your own argument about the **literary value** of media texts.

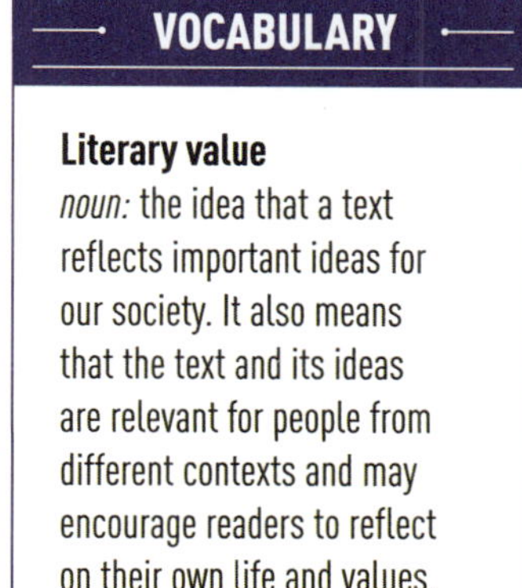

VOCABULARY

Literary value
noun: the idea that a text reflects important ideas for our society. It also means that the text and its ideas are relevant for people from different contexts and may encourage readers to reflect on their own life and values.

4.11.4 Understanding and responding to texts C

Consider media in its broader sense: the method of mass communication via platforms like the internet, television and radio.

What value do you think the media has in our world today? Explain with references to popular examples, if possible.

____

____

____

____

____

Despite the need to question and assess the credibility and authority of media texts, there is value in having so many opinions and perspectives communicated on a large scale. Different versions of the 'truth' can help audiences challenge their existing beliefs and values, be exposed to new ways of seeing the world, and consider how a topic impacts people from diverse groups. Let's see this in action.

4.11.5 Reading, viewing and listening to texts

1 Choose a topic that has been represented in the media in recent times. You may be inspired by some of these topics.

Artificial intelligence	Homelessness	Australia Day
Women in sport	Changes to the 9:00–3:00 school day	Teen mental health

My chosen topic: ______________________________

2 Search for three media texts that each present a different view on this topic. Texts may include feature articles, social media posts, online videos, television segments and advertisements.

Record the name of the text and a summary of how it presents the topic you have chosen.

Media text 1	Media text 2	Media text 3

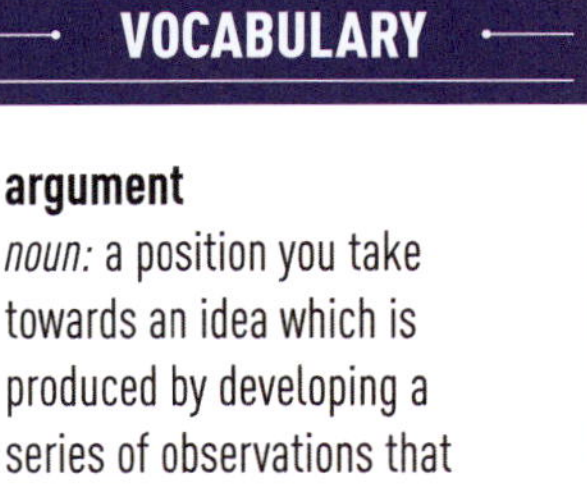

VOCABULARY

argument
noun: a position you take towards an idea which is produced by developing a series of observations that support an overall position

Texts use **argument** to add to their authority on a topic. Constructing and maintaining an argument can give a text authority, both in the way it positions audiences to respond to the text and in constructing its own credibility in dealing with a topic. The feature articles you examined earlier in this chapter demonstrate this in written form, as they present arguments on topics and provide paragraphs that develop ideas. However, texts in other forms of media also use their codes and conventions to construct and develop arguments. For example, a print advertisement may emphasise certain parts of an image to reflect their importance, and social media videos may use a combination of sound, visuals and text to highlight their stance on a topic.

4.11.6 Understanding and responding to texts B

Select one of the media texts on your chosen topic that you selected for the previous activity. Examine how an argument is constructed to give this text authority.

1 What argument does this text present on the topic?

____

____

____

2 What supporting ideas does the text give to develop this argument?

____

____

____

3 How do the features of the text work together to construct this argument?

____

____

____

4 How do you think the argument of this text impacts its authority?

____

____

____

4.11.7 Expressing ideas and composing texts A

Now it is your turn to create your own argument. You will create a written text that presents an argument about the value of these diverse representations of your chosen topic, by responding to this question: *What is the value of media texts that present different views on the topic of*

______________________________?

Create an extended written text that presents your argument about the value of how three media texts reflect different views on your chosen topic.

Media, media, everywhere!

1 Plan your response.

Topic:	
Argument: What is the value of having different views on this topic presented? What do audiences gain from these varied representations?	
Media text 1: What is the value of this text? How does it create authority on this topic??	
Media text 2: What is the value of this text? How does it create authority on this topic?	
Media text 3: What is the value of this text? How does it create authority on this topic?	

2 Examine the structure below to help you construct your written argument.

Introduction →
- Introduce the chosen topic.
- Introduce the three media texts.
- Outline your argument about the value of different views in these texts.

Body paragraph 1 →
- Outline a point about the value of **Media text 1** in understanding the topic.
- Explain how the text uses language to create authority.

Body paragraph 2 →
- Outline a point about the value of **Media text 2** in understanding the topic.
- Explain how the text uses language to create authority.

Body paragraph 3 →
- Outline a point about the value of **Media text 3** in understanding the topic.
- Explain how the text uses language to create authority.

Conclusion
- Outline what audiences can gain from the diverse ideas presented through these media texts.
- Draw a conclusion about the value of media in our world.

3 Consider the language you will use to convey your argument. Circle the types of language from the list that you plan to use. If you are unfamiliar with any of the types of language look them up online.

Rhetorical questions	Evaluative language	Comparative language
Hyperbole	Emotive language	Active and/or passive voice

4 Write your response here to the question *What is the value of media texts that present different views on the topic of* ______________________?

4.11.8 Chapter reflection

1 Do you think there any media texts that are free from bias? Explain your response.

2 What is the relationship between argument and authority? Refer to a text you've engaged with in this chapter to support your ideas.

3 Let's return to this unit's inquiry question: ***How do media texts have authority over their audience, and can they be trusted to present the truth?*** How have your learning and reading experiences in chapter 11 addressed the inquiry question?

CHAPTER 12: INTERACTIVE ENGAGEMENT

Chapter overview

In this final chapter of the unit, you will explore how the authorship of media texts like social media, podcasts and interactive websites is both collaborative and dynamic. You will examine the role the audience plays, as an active participant in media texts, in constructing authority. You will also consider the digital footprints that audiences leave behind from their engagement with this type of media. You will develop arguments about the role of interactivity in media texts for modern audiences by exploring how codes and conventions of digital texts are combined to produce immersive and engaging experiences.

Success criteria: in this chapter, I will be successful when I can ...

- describe how some media texts have acquired mass followings and altered the landscape of media
- explain how the codes and conventions of media texts can be used to create interactive and immersive digital texts
- analyse the extent to which authorship of media texts is collaborative
- compose arguments that develop personal opinions about the relationship between media texts and their audiences.

Chapter inquiry questions

- What role do audiences of social media play in creating authority?
- How important is interactivity in digital texts for modern audiences?

Key vocabulary

- social media
- authorship
- collaborative
- viral
- trending
- digital footprint
- interactivity
- active participant

What role do audiences of social media play in creating authority?

There is no doubt that **social media** has authority in our world. There are a significant number of social media applications that Australians engage with every day. Some are for personal use, others are for business, and some blur the line between personal and public use.

VOCABULARY

social media
noun: refers to websites and applications that allow users to create and share content in a social, interactive environment.

4.12.1 Warm-up

Social media survey

1 In small groups, create a list of all the social media applications that you use frequently (at least once a week). For each application, identify the method of communication (that is, messaging, text, images) and discuss what you like and dislike about the application.

2 Discuss each of the following statements in relation to social media.

I am in control of what I see on social media.

Social media is fun.

Social media is just part of life now; it's our primary method of communication.

If I'm not paying to use the application, I am most likely the 'product' of the application.

Using social media makes me more informed about the world.

The audience of social media is just the consumer.

3 Choose one of the statements and explain your response to it.

In chapter 10, you learned that one meaning of authority refers to who controls the meaning of a text. So who are the 'authors' in the world of social media? Is it the person who creates a post and shares it online? Is it the audience who likes the post and shares it with others? Or is it really the technology company that designed and programs the social media application itself? Perhaps authority comes from all of these parties involved in social media. Perhaps authority is collaborative.

Let's look at an example of this. In 2020, the media outlet SBS set up a fake Instagram account called @thatcoastalgirl. It curated an image of an easygoing young woman interested in wellness and living a coastal lifestyle. After the creators bought 2,500 'followers' for the account, @thatcoastalgirl was approached by businesses to promote their products and services.

Use the QR code below to access the website The Feed: Faking influence *and learn more about this case study.*

4.12.2 Understanding and responding to texts B

1 What was the aim of the fake Instagram account?

2 What have you learned about the way social media is used to promote businesses and products?

3 How does this case study show that the authorship of social media is collaborative?

4.12.3 Expressing ideas and composing texts A

Fake yourself!

Create a series of six images on the Instagram grid below that present a carefully curated image of you. Choose an aspect of yourself to exaggerate, or make up an entirely new version of yourself. You may include drawings, images or text in each image.

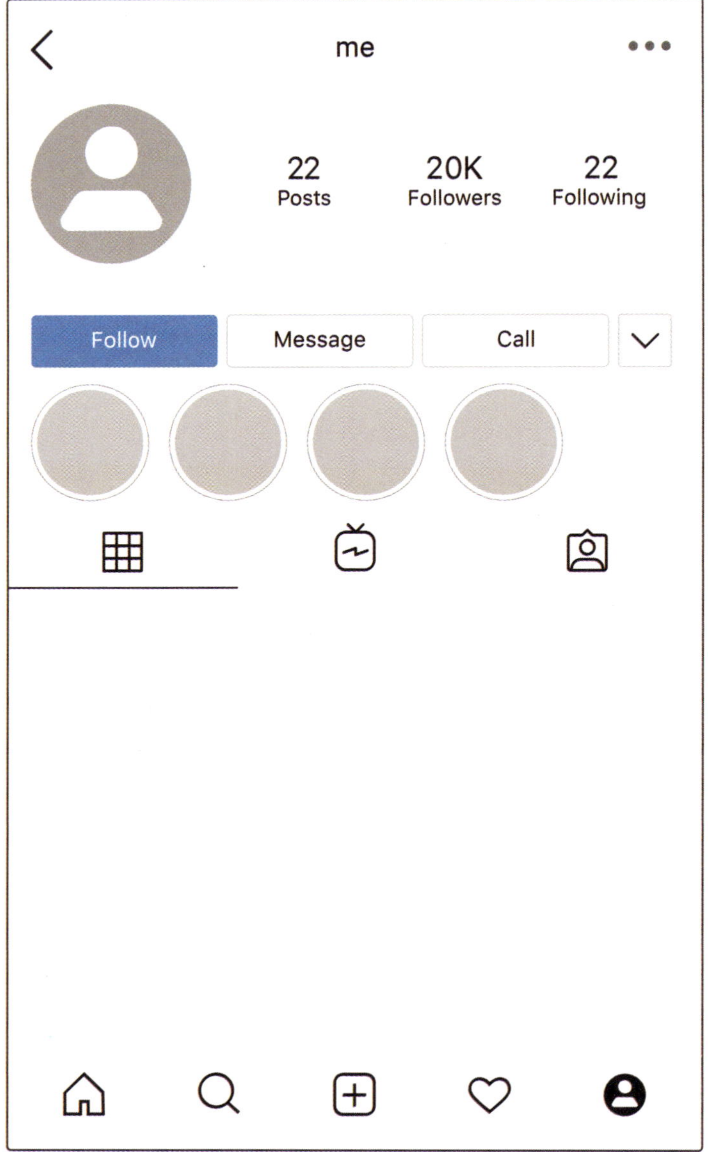

If you are a user of social media, you will have heard the term 'gone **viral**'. This occurs when a social media post becomes extremely popular and accumulates a large number of interactions quickly, such as likes, shares and views. Another term you may have heard in the world of social media is '**trending**'. Like going viral, trending occurs when topics, hashtags or keywords become popular on social media. Trends also go as quickly as they appear, as audiences move on to another trend.

Some say there is no rhyme or reason to which type of content goes viral or trends. However, the content usually induces a strong psychological response (that is, a strong feeling) in audiences, and audiences are usually compelled by a social motivation to share the post (for example, to share something funny, cute or clever with their friends, or to support a social justice movement).

Regardless of the reason, viral content shows us that **authorship** of social media is **collaborative**, as meaning is attributed to the content when it is interacted with by audiences. Interestingly, social media trends can also start to become part of 'real-life' society, as talk moves from online platforms to the real world.

Businesses can also take advantage of social media to create trends to promote their products and services. Find and view some of the viral social media marketing campaigns listed below. Consider why audiences engaged with these campaigns strongly enough to make them go viral.

- Ice Bucket Challenge – the ALS Association
- Bring Back the Moustache – Movember Foundation
- You Never Lamb Alone – Meat And Livestock Australia
- Earth Hour – World Wildlife Fund
- So where the bloody hell are you? – Tourism Australia

4.12.4 Understanding and responding to texts C

Select one viral campaign from the list and answer these questions.

1 **What was the aim of the campaign?**

____

____

2 **Why do you think this campaign went viral? Consider psychological responses and social motivation.**

____

____

____

____

3 What does the popularity of this viral campaign reflect about our society?

Another way in which the authority of social media is collaborative is the role that social media applications themselves play in controlling what we see and interact with online. Read this extract from an article published by *The Conversation* about the algorithms used by social media applications.

Feed me: 4 ways to take control of social media algorithms and get the content you actually want

Marc Cheong, 11 May 2023

Whether it's Facebook's News Feed or TikTok's For You page, social media algorithms are constantly making behind-the-scenes decisions to boost certain content – giving rise to the 'curated' feeds we've all become accustomed to.

... In broader computing terms, an algorithm is simply a set of rules that specifies a particular computational procedure.

In a social media context, algorithms (specifically 'recommender algorithms') determine everything from what you're likely to read, to whom you're likely to follow, to whether a specific post appears in front of you.

Their main goal is to sustain your attention for as long as possible, in a process called 'optimising for engagement'. The more you engage with content on a platform, the more effectively that platform can commodify your attention and target you with ads: its main revenue source.

... Imagine a hypothetical user named Basil who follows users and pages that primarily discuss *space*, *dog memes* and *cooking*. Social media algorithms might give Basil recommendations for T-shirts featuring puppies dressed as astronauts.

Although this might seem simple, algorithms are typically 'black boxes' that have their inner workings hidden. It's in the interests of tech companies to keep the recipe for their 'secret sauce', well, a secret.

... TikTok's algorithm, in particular, is notoriously powerful yet opaque. A Wall Street Journal investigation found it uses 'subtle cues, such as how long you linger on a video' to predict what you're likely to engage with.

4.12.5 Expressing ideas and composing texts A

From your reading about the algorithms used by social media applications and the way audiences can make social media content go viral, create an argument that responds to this statement: *There are no single authors in the world of social media; instead, authority is collaborative.*

Due to the collaborative nature of authority in media texts, it is more important than ever to consider the way in which you ethically and responsibly engage with social media. A '**digital footprint**' is the information that exists about you on the internet as a result of your online activity. Your digital footprint may have implications for your safety, education or future career.

In a world where so many details of our lives are shared on social media, the line between what is personal and public is sometimes difficult to determine, particularly for those who hold positions of responsibility in the community.

Read this extract from another article published by The Conversation *in the* USA.

School board members could soon be blocked from blocking people – and deleting their comments – on social media

Charles J. Russo, 5 January 2024

If a school board member has a social media account, would it be wrong for them to block someone and delete their comments? That's a question the Supreme Court has decided to take up after public officials, including two school board members, blocked constituents from seeing their accounts or removed critical comments.

At stake is what constitutes state action – or action taken in an official governmental capacity – on social media. Under the First Amendment, officials engaging in state action cannot restrict individuals' freedom of speech and expression.

A ruling in the case, likely to come in spring or early summer 2024, could have broad implications for American society, where nearly three-fourths of the population use social media in their daily lives. The ruling could also establish whether social media accounts of public officials should be treated as personal or governmental.

DISCUSS

After reading the article, discuss the following in a small group.

› What do you know about the term 'freedom of speech'? Is posting anything online an example of this?

› Research the laws in Australia that force social media companies to name users who bully others or post harmful content. Do you believe this is enough to ensure that people use social media appropriately?

4.12.6 Expressing ideas and composing texts A

A person should be able to share whatever they like using their personal social media account.

Write a paragraph that presents an argument in response to the statement above. In your paragraph you must include:

- a thesis statement that outlines your position in response to the statement
- examples from your reading in this chapter to support your position
- cause-and-effect language that shows how the evidence you have selected supports your argument
- evaluative language that makes a judgement to support your position in response to the statement.

How important is interactivity in digital texts for modern audiences?

As you learned in chapter 10, media texts are driven by the need to seize and maintain audience attention. A significant part of gaining this attention in digital texts is the level of **interactivity** offered by the text for audiences to become **active participants** in the reading, viewing or listening experience.

This diagram shows how some of the codes and conventions of digital texts invite users to become active participants in their use.

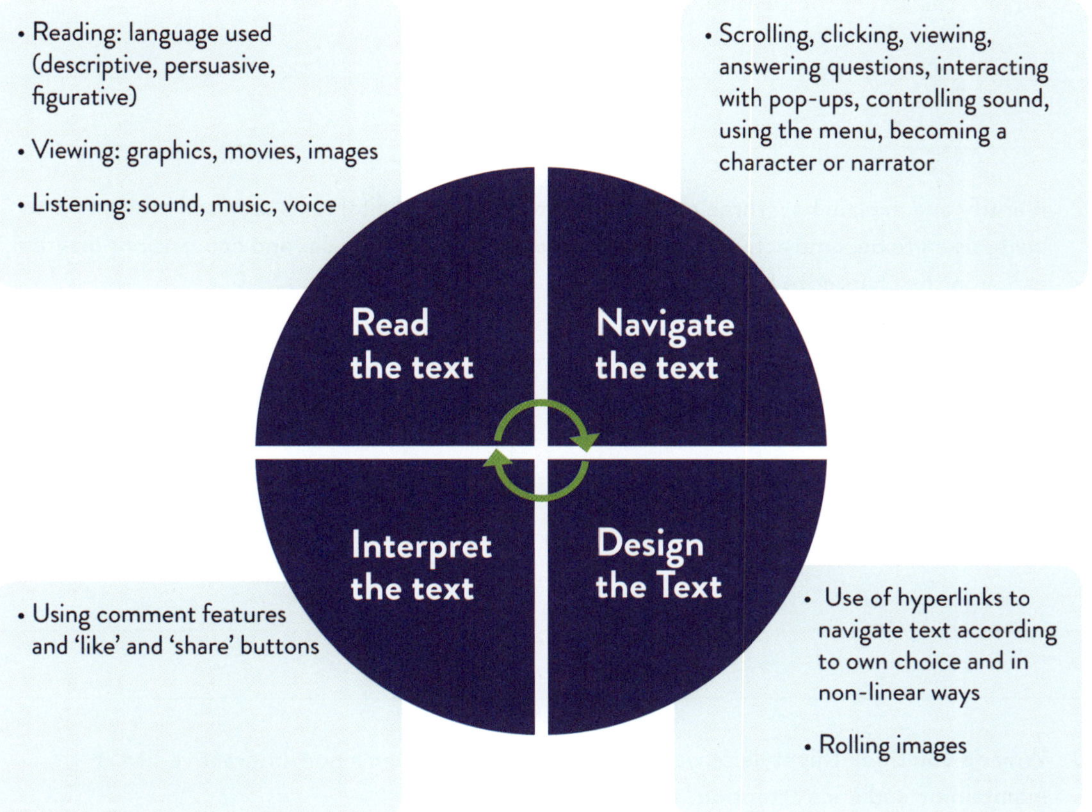

This kind of interactivity is even used in the way we access and consume news coverage, information about geographical locations or content about particular issues.

Use the QR code to access Beneath the Waves, *an interactive documentary on the Western Australian Museum website. Explore the ways in which interactive elements are used to gain the attention of the audience.*

4.12.7 Understanding and responding to texts A

Access and view the following websites. When you have explored them all, select one website and respond to the questions that follow.

K'gari	*Beneath the Blue*	*I'm Your Man*	*The Boat*

1 What is the aim of the website?

2 Identify and explain how three codes and conventions of digital texts are used in this text to invite users to become active participants. (Look again at the codes and conventions diagram earlier in the chapter to help you.)

3 Why do you think this style of website is more effective than a non-interactive site at maintaining audience attention?

Another popular form of digital text is a podcast. A podcast is a series of spoken conversations focused on a particular topic or theme. Although they are audio texts, podcasts are accessed digitally, making them digital texts.

Podcasts rely on interactivity between the host/s and the audience even though only one side has an actual voice. In this form, interactivity relies on discussing ideas from the podcast with others, sharing the podcast on social media, and engaging with other listeners of the podcast via comment features or forums.

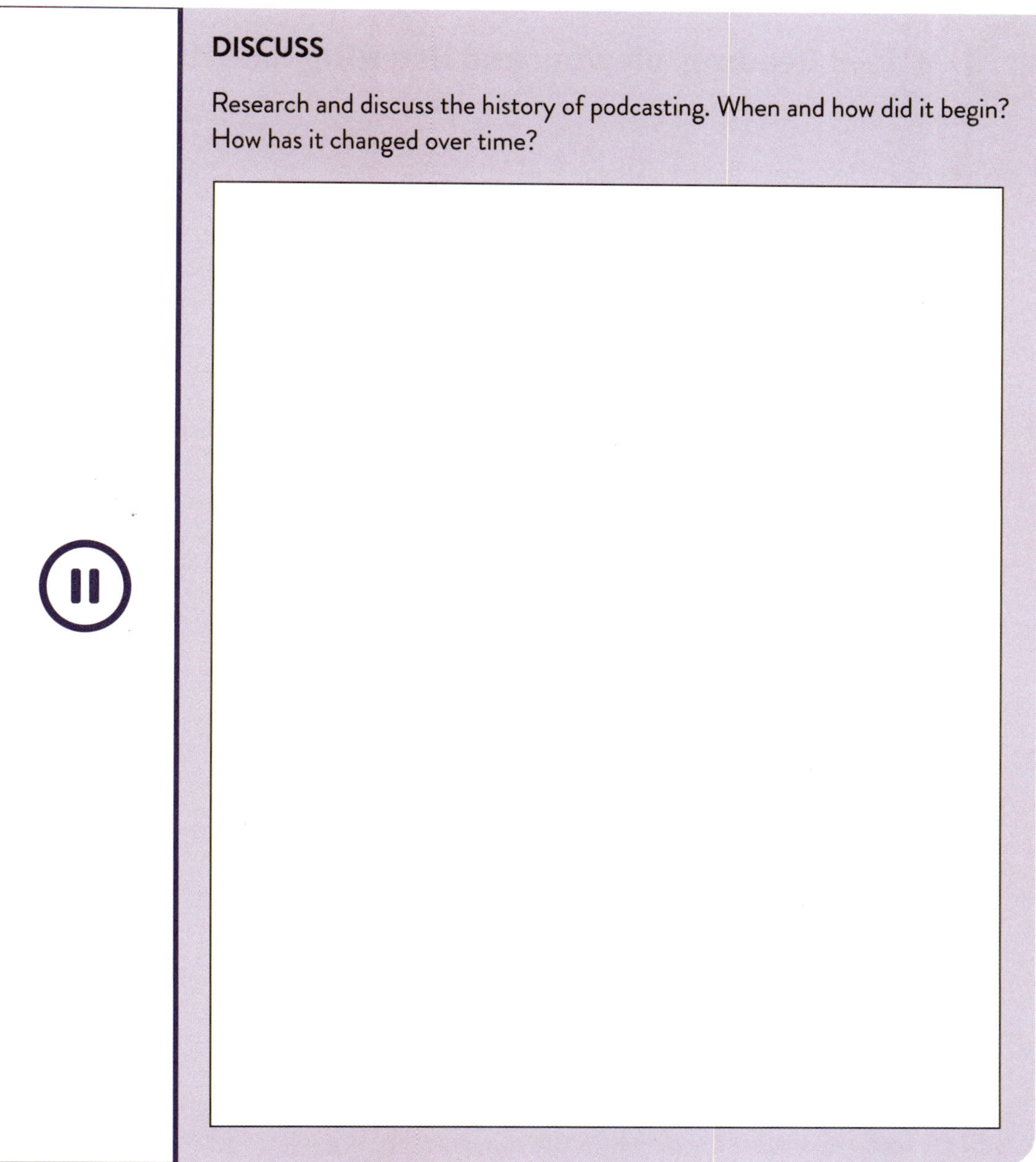

Find an episode of one of these podcasts online and listen to it.

- *Short & Curly*
- *Fierce Girls*
- *The Unexplainable Disappearance of Mars Patel*
- *Sleek Geeks*
- *WOW in the World*

4.12.8 Reading, viewing and listening to texts

1 What did you like about this podcast episode?

2 How do the creators of the podcast use a range of features to maintain audience attention?

3 In what ways are listeners invited to interact with this podcast?

4.12.9 Chapter reflection

1 What further ideas have you learned about the authority of media texts in this chapter?

2 If you are a user of digital texts or social media, what has this chapter challenged you to think about in the way you use this technology?

3 Let's return to this unit's inquiry question: ***How do media texts have authority over their audience, and can they be trusted to present the truth?*** How have your learning and reading experiences in Chapter 12 addressed the inquiry question?

Unit 4: Summative assessment

The summative assessment options below provide opportunities to demonstrate your achievement of the following outcomes and content points.

Outcome and focus area	EN4-RVL-01 Reading, viewing and listening to texts	EN4-URA-01 Understanding and responding to texts A	EN4-URB-01 Understanding and responding to texts B	EN4-URC-01 Understanding and responding to texts C	EN4-ECA-01 Expressing ideas and composing texts A
Content point	Reading, viewing and listening skills Reading, viewing and listening for meaning	Code and convention	Argument and authority	Literary value	Speaking Text features: persuasive

Option 1:

Write an extended response that develops an argument in response to the Unit 4 inquiry question, *How do media texts have authority over their audience, and can they be trusted to present the truth?*

Ensure that your response:
- provides an idea about the way **authority** is constructed in media texts
- refers to examples of media texts to support ideas, closely examining how the **codes and conventions** of the texts are used to create authority
- considers the **value** and role of media texts in our modern world
- logically sequences ideas to develop an **argument**.

Option 2:

In groups of three, prepare your team's case for a formal debate in response to this statement: *Social media companies should be held responsible for fake news and misinformation that is spread on their platforms.*

If there are enough teams that have opposing views, perhaps the debates could be held in class. Ensure that your team's response to the statement considers:
- the way **authority** is constructed in media texts
- relevant examples of media texts to support ideas, closely examining how the **codes and conventions** of the texts are used to create authority
- the **value** and role of media texts in our modern world
- how to logically sequences ideas to develop an **argument**.

Option 3:

You and a partner are the hosts of a new podcast called *Media Matters* which explores the value and role of media texts in our world. Each episode focuses on a different way in which media texts contribute to society and the role audiences play in responding to these texts.

Write and record one episode of the podcast. Give your episode a title that reflects your overall argument.

Ensure that your podcast episode:

- provides an idea about the way **authority** is constructed in media texts
- refers to examples of media texts to support ideas, closely examining how the **codes and conventions** of the texts are used to create authority
- considers the **value** and role of media texts in our modern world
- logically sequences ideas to develop an **argument**.

Assessment as learning: self-assessment

Does my response:

- ☐ discuss the authority of media texts?
- ☐ refer to relevant examples of media texts and their use of codes and conventions?
- ☐ evaluate the value of media texts in our modern world?
- ☐ logically sequence and develop ideas to support the overall argument?

What are two strengths of my response?

____

____

What area/s of my response do I need to refine further?

____

____

____

____

ACKNOWLEDGEMENTS

Insight Publications thanks the author, Emily Beach, for her work on *English for NSW, Year 8, Stage 4*.

Insight Publications is also grateful to the following individuals and organisations for permission to reproduce copyright material.

Texts: English K-10 Syllabus © NSW Education Standards Authority for and on behalf of the Crown in right of the State of New South Wales, 2012; Extract: *Dragon Hunter* by Nazam Anhar © Nazam Anhar; Extracts: Text © 2011 Patrick Ness , From an original idea by Siobhan Dowd , Illustrations © 2011 Jim Kay , **From A MONSTER CALLS, Written by Patrick Ness & Illustrated by Jim Kay** , Reproduced by permission of Walker Books Ltd, London, SE11 5HJ , www.walker.co.uk; Extract: *Harry Potter and the Philosopher's Stone* © J.K. Rowling, 1997, reproduced with permission from The Blair Partnership; Extract: The *Woman in Black* by Susan Hill, Penguin Random House; Extract: *Turtles All the Way Down* by John Green, Penguin Random House; Maya Angelou, 'Still I Rise' from *And Still I Rise*: A Book of Poems, © 1978 by Maya Angelou, reproduced with permission of the Licensor through PLSclear; Extract: 'The Battle' by Tara Finn – from *Nearly Impossible Dreams & other Poems* by Tara Finn, Green Olive Press; Extract: *The War that Saved My Life* by Kimberly Brubaker Bradley, Text Publishing; 'Climate March' from *It's the Sound of the Thing*, text and illustration © 2023 Maxine Beneba Clarke, first published in Australia by Hardie Grant Children's Publishing; Extract: *Runt* by Craig Silvey, Allen and Unwin; Extract: '16th birthday speech to the United Nations' by Malala Yousafzai; 'The Hill We Climb' by Amanda Gorman © Amanda Gorman; Extract: *Sister Heart* by Sally Morgan, Fremantle Press; Extract: *Honey Spot* by Jack Davis, Currency Press; Extract: *The Boy from the Mish* by Gary Lonesborough, 2021, Allen&Unwin; Extract: *Talking To My Country* by Stan Grant, Harper Collins Australia; Extract: THE INTERROGATION OF ASHALA WOLF by Ambelin Kwaymullina Text © 2012 Ambelin Kwaymullina , reproduced by permission of Walker Books Australia Pty Ltd; Extract: reprinted from *Terra Nullius* by Claire Coleman, Hachette Australia, 2017; *The Conversation*, 'Feed me: 4 ways to take control of social media algorithms and get the content you actually want' by Marc Cheong, The University of Melbourne; *The Conversation*, 'School board members could soon be blocked from blocking people – and deleting their comments – on social media' by Charles J. Russo, University of Dayton.

Images: E. Phillips Fox 'Landing of Captain Cook at Botany Bay', 1770 1902, oil on canvas, 192.2 × 265.4 cm, National Gallery of Victoria, Melbourne, Gilbee Bequest, 1902, Photo: National Gallery of Victoria, Melbourne; 'We Call Them Pirates Out Here' by Daniel Boyd (2006), ©Daniel Boyd; Images reproduced with permission from *The Rabbits* by Shaun Tan and John Marsden, Hachette Australia, 2010; The following images from Alamy: various screenshots from the film 'Lion' by Garth Davis; Additional images from Shutterstock.